Southern Literary Studies
Fred Hobson, Editor

HORTON FOOTE and the
Theater of Intimacy

HORTON FOOTE and the Theater of Intimacy

GERALD C. WOOD

Louisiana State University Press

Baton Rouge

Copyright © 1999 by Louisiana State University Press
All rights reserved
Manufactured in the United States of America
First printing
08 07 06 05 04 03 02 01 00 99   5 4 3 2 1

Designer: Amanda McDonald Scallan
Typeface: Galliard
Typesetter: Coghill Composition Company, Inc.
Printer and binder: Edwards Brothers, Inc.

Library of Congress Cataloging-in-Publication Data

Wood, Gerald C.
    Horton Foote and the theater of intimacy / Gerald C. Wood.
      p. cm.—(Southern literary studies)
    Includes bibliographical references and index.
    ISBN 0-8071-2295-5 (cloth : alk. paper)
    1. Foote, Horton—Criticism and interpretation. 2. Drama—
Psychological aspects. 3. Drama—Religious aspects. 4. Texas—In
literature. I. Title. II. Series.
    PS3511.0344Z95 1999
     812'.54—dc21   99-14902
                                                CIP

The paper in this book meets the guidelines for permanence and durability of the Committee on Production Guidelines for Book Longevity of the Council on Library Resources.⊗

Some chapters of this book originally appeared, in slightly different form, in the following publications
and are reprinted with the permission of the editors: chapter 4 as "Horton Foote's Politics of Intimacy,"
in *Journal of American Drama and Theatre,* Spring 1997; chapter 5 as "Old Beginnings and Roads to
Home: Horton Foote and Mythic Realism," in *Christianity and Literature,* Spring–Summer 1996; and
chapter 8 as "The Nature of Mystery in *The Young Man from Atlanta,*" in *Horton Foote: A Casebook,* ed.
Gerald C. Wood (New York: Garland Press, 1998).

For my parents,

my children,

and

Leonard Handler

"Boo was our neighbor. He gave us two soap dolls, a broken watch and chain, a knife, and our lives."

—*To Kill a Mockingbird*

Contents

Contents

Acknowledgments

The initial research for this study was funded by a James Still Fellowship and a travel stipend, both from the Appalachian College Program at the University of Kentucky. The PEW Foundation, through a grant to Carson-Newman College, and Bryan Tours supported leaves for writing and travel. In the final months of my research, the Appalachian College Association, under the leadership of Alice Brown and John Hennen, granted me a John B. Stephenson Fellowship (from the Mellon Foundation) for revision of the manuscript.

At Carson-Newman College, Larry Osborne, past dean of Academic Special Programs; Mike Carter, provost; and Cordell Maddox, president, continually supported this project, as did Lynda Hill and Carolyn Petty, Becky Boatright and Chris Rhodes, Maria Dorman, Shara Whitford, Pat Brown, Jennifer Corum, Anjanette Large, Nichole Stewart, and especially Angela Ellis Roberts. Students in three courses on Horton Foote (including my colleague Don Garner) shared their insights into much of the material covered in this book. In Wharton, Texas, Eve Barlett and the Wharton Museum were very helpful in securing pictures and articles from local and regional newspapers, and Kelly Kline, Foote's secretary, has always made my connections to Wharton easy and clear. Mary Hunter Wolf kindly offered a fascinating interview—and a good lunch—in New Haven, Connecticut. Thanks, too, to the artists interviewed for the *Tender Mercies* chapter, as well as Martin Marty, Ralph Wood, John May, James Wall, Kimball King, Chuck Maland, and Fred Hobson for their timely and excellent advice on publication. At LSU John Easterly, Gerry Anders, and Mimi Bhattacharyya offered expert criticism and suggestions.

The Fred Coe Collection in the television and film archives at the University of Wisconsin, Madison, and the Museum of Broadcasting in New York granted access to early Foote television material. And the DeGolyer Library at Southern Methodist University—David Farmer, director, and Kay Bost, curator of Archives, Manuscripts, and Photographs—was most attentive to permissions, copying, and every detail when I studied the Horton Foote Papers in the summer of 1995.

Lillian and Horton Foote were very helpful during the preparation of this manuscript, especially in granting permission to read from the private papers before those were placed at SMU; without that trip to Wharton, my work would be incomplete. And to their children—Barbara Hallie, Horton, Walter, and Daisy—thanks for interviews, a few nights' lodging, copying, advice, and a bad round or two of golf.

Most of all, I thank my children—Tim and Sarah Wood—for their patience and understanding. Enthusiastic fans of Foote's work, they tolerated my distractions and absences while I wrote and revised this study. I love you for this and many other reasons.

HORTON FOOTE and the

Theater of Intimacy

1

The Playwright, Dialectical Writing, and Intimacy

Horton Foote is recognized as one of America's most talented screen-writers. This judgment is based, in part, on his two Academy Awards. His 1962 screen version of Harper Lee's novel *To Kill a Mockingbird* won the Oscar for best adaptation, and in 1983 his work on *Tender Mercies* was voted best original screenplay. To those who follow film closely, Foote is known for writing *The Trip to Bountiful,* the 1988 film that earned him another Oscar nomination and Geraldine Page her only Academy Award, and for *Baby, the Rain Must Fall,* a 1964 Alan Pakula/Robert Mulligan adaptation of the writer's own play *The Traveling Lady.* Students of independent film probably know *Tomorrow* (1972), starring Robert Duvall, a classic adaptation of a William Faulkner story, as well as Foote's mid-1980s independent films from his play cycle *The Orphans' Home.* His 1992 adaptation of John Steinbeck's *Of Mice and Men* for Gary Sinise also was widely distributed.

In addition to film aficionados, an equally appreciative group of the-atergoers considers Foote a major playwright. They would not be surprised to learn that since he first wrote for the American Actors Company in the late 1930s, more than forty of his plays have been produced, most of them in New York or Washington, D.C. Followers of regional theater have attended recent productions of his work in Los Angeles, Louisville, Cleveland, Houston, Dallas, Winston-Salem, Pittsburgh, Sarasota, Chapel Hill, and Montgomery. He earned the Ensemble Studio Theatre Founders Award in 1985 and the Compostela Award in 1988. In 1995 he won a number of awards, including the Lucille Lortel Award and the Pulitzer Prize for *The Young Man from Atlanta*.

Students of television know of Foote's contributions to the golden age of that medium in the mid-1950s. Both *Bountiful* and *Baby, the Rain Must Fall* appeared on TV, and other Foote teleplays—among them *The Travelers*, *Expectant Relations*, *Flight*, *A Young Lady of Property*, *The Midnight Caller*, *John Turner Davis*, and *The Dancers*—were major productions of early television. Students of the small screen realize that, often nurtured by producer Fred Coe, these plays are ranked with those of Paddy Chayefsky and Gore Vidal as among the best drama of their time. When television drama was frequently live, Horton Foote's work was recognized by his colleagues as personal and exceptional.

A number of biographical discussions have chronicled Foote's achievements in film, theater, and television. His early work as an actor in Texas, California, and the New York City area has been noted, and the influence of Mary Hunter, Agnes de Mille, and the American Actors Company has been described, as has Foote's experimental work in dance and theater throughout the 1940s. In interviews he has restated his motives for spending the second half of that decade as a teacher, director, and producer in Washington, D.C. The writer has also answered questions about his work in early television—including *The Gabby Hayes Show*—his first commissioned writing for the movies, and his retreat from the stage in the 1960s and 1970s. He has recounted his few happy experiences in Hollywood and his many unsatisfying ones. Finally, his return to the stage with *The Orphans' Home* cycle and his recent successful efforts as an independent filmmaker have been duly recorded.

Critics attempting to explain Foote's success often have apologized, in one way or another, for the writer's use of his homeplace—Wharton, Texas. Foote has been considered a Texas writer, an east Texas writer, a Gulf Coast writer, and (more accurately) a coastal southeast Texas writer. His use of the Texas idiom is sometimes considered a strength; at other times it is seen as limiting. For some of his detractors, Foote's interest in

Texas and religious values is judged too southern and sentimental. For his admirers, his stoic, understated characters, his tendency to dedramatize, and his rich subtexts express the best of his Lone Star heritage. It has become easy to name Foote a Texas bard.

The tendency to describe Horton Foote as a regional writer can, however, be very misleading, for it reduces his work to local color and misinterprets, for example, his attitudes toward personal responsibility, the family, and the past. While generally faithful to his region, Foote uses his stories to fashion a distinctive artistry for both theater and film. His characters—even those from outside coastal southeast Texas—typically speak in a shortened, compressed language that hides as much as it reveals. And when they do open up to themselves and others, expression is powerfully restrained. The author seldom allows his characters, or even his audience, to indulge in these moments of revelation. In the Foote canon, although more pointedly in his later works, emotional growth is very subtle, hardly public, and most often a matter of the subtext, not the text, of the story. This aspect of his work can be the most difficult, for the stories often quietly respond to one another, offering variations on their common themes. No single play is quintessential Foote.

This dialectical method results from the author's basic commitment to writing as a process, a way of continuously engaging and understanding the world. He says he wants "to get people to reexamine and to think about each other and relationships and the lives we live." But writing should not be moralistic; his readers and audiences should "decide for themselves. Being didactic doesn't interest me." And so he creates, he hopes, a participatory art: "I'm always trying to change my point of view, to see something fresh, to understand and to present what I perceive, and to engage whoever is watching in that process." Despite its often old-fashioned look, Foote's drama requires a most contemporary spirit of discovery, what Marc Robinson calls the "act of looking for . . . not a showing off of what has been seen."[1]

Foote's point of view is open and self-renewing; his work is neither diffuse nor chaotic. As he clarified in a recent interview for *Post Script,* "If I have a vision, I don't sit down and plan it. If I have a vision, it's uncon-

1. Amanda Smith, "Horton Foote: A Writer's Journey," *Varia,* I (July–August 1987), 27; Marc Robinson, *The Other American Drama* (New York, 1994), 180.

3

scious. . . . I mean something asserts itself out of my own sense of living."[2] Although Foote's vision is never fully realized in a single work because of his reliance on art-as-discovery, it is nevertheless remarkably coherent. His earliest unpublished plays are about going away and coming home, and his teleplays describe grief, healing, and the eternal quest for peace and contentment. His commissioned work, too, praises flexibility and courage. Read together, Foote's plays and screenplays—produced and unproduced—reveal an artist on a personal journey to the heart of modern American loneliness.

As the following chapters explain, of primary concern for Horton Foote as a man and writer is the absence of love in modern American society. Love, however, is too general and rhetorical to be the subject of his art. More interested in relationships than ideas, experience than truth, Foote's work for stage and film focuses on whether his isolated characters can connect meaningfully with the confusing, violent, and transitory world around them—that is, whether they can find and nurture intimacy in its many forms. Usually, and most obviously, his characters feel supported and inspired by parents, mates, and children. Additionally, some discover that the land, their work, a community, or religion offers a magical point of contact. With intimacy—the active expression of love—violence disappears, and courage and freedom are possible.

Integral to this intimacy is the deeply felt erotic nature of human experience; Foote's women and men are driven by powerful physical needs. But he also maintains that desire can be confusing and destructive if it is not shaped by personal choice and public ritual. For the writer's lonely characters, neediness and eros make dangerous bedfellows. In Foote's plays, healthy sexuality always leads to deep understanding, friendship, and commitment—the only satisfying forms of intimacy. These two primary impulses—the erotic and the familial—meet in the dance, Foote's metaphor for the proper balance between passion and order.

The crisis Foote describes is reflected in failed families, lost religious moorings, confusion in the workplace and bedroom. But Foote is not reactionary; a humanist at heart, he is careful to note the point of view, burdens, and choices of his characters. Always sympathetic to his creations, the author investigates a profound narcissism that alienates his people

2. Gerald C. Wood, "Horton Foote: An Interview," *Post Script*, X (Summer 1991), 10.

from history and tradition. With little sense of their place in nature, society, or religion, they lack identity and purpose. Without nurturing ties to others, courage and responsibility are elusive, and empathy, comfort, and healing become impossible. Sickened by chronic feelings of emotional and spiritual emptiness, Foote's characters desperately need affection and affiliation.

This hunger for intimacy helps explain Foote's obsessive interest in place, the subject of chapter 2. Despite its coastal southeast Texas setting, the writer's world is both imaginary and personal. Scruffy prairies and dry, parched ground become metaphors for a life without connection and love, and the Texas bottomlands represent an eternal need for nurturing and groundedness. In this fictional landscape characters are drawn to symbols of rootedness: trees and homes. When achieved, intimacy is hard won and, in a world governed by time, never eternal. As a result, most people live on the thresholds, unaware that their lives enact Foote's drama of going away and coming home. Their struggle for identity, like the writer's own need to create, is imagined as an eternal longing for a home. This home is never a literal place or thing of the past. It is the feeling that comes from connectedness to families, work, a community, a religious belief.

Discovering a sense of place, being intimately attached to a tradition greater than oneself, is often fostered by the grounding presence of special women. This female spirit, the topic of chapter 3, begins with the capacity of certain Foote women to feel and share the primary forces of life. More aware than men of the rhythms of living and dying, they manage their emotions by loving others more than themselves. These saintly women accept life beyond their control; they assert themselves when needed, but they also celebrate mystery. Their courage heals orphaned characters, especially the men, by transforming the leaden material world into a graceful spiritual one. Benevolent presences, these women—and the spirit they represent—offer the assurance that intimacy is real.

Belief, often inspired by these women, is a source of hope and courage in Foote's fictional world. The writer does not assert his own religious point of view in the text of his work. Nor is he didactic. Rather, religion is meant to offer order and direction in times of rootlessness and disintegration. While his believers are not spared from their personal demons or social injustice, religion can encourage the sense of self to which these characters unconsciously aspire. Foote should thus be included with the late-twentieth-century American writers who, according to C. W. E. Bigsby in his survey of American drama since World War II, have rediscovered "spiritualism": "The failure of ideology to inform or shape the world satisfactorily, of psychology convincingly to offer a secular route to self-understanding, or self-interest, of materialism or the rituals of social form to offer a structure to experience or a destination worthy of the journey, left them standing at the doors of faith."[3] Faith, while never insisted upon, is the most sustaining path to freedom in Horton Foote's theater of intimacy.

As he creates a mental and religious theater which studies the nature of courage and freedom, Foote does not avoid social contexts in his call for intimacy. His desire for genuine and nourishing attachments is complicated, and often made impossible, by the indifference and injustice that haunts the Texas landscape. Whether historical or contemporary, his dramas are marked by infidelity, sexism, racism, insanity, and murder. What gives them a distinctive voice, characteristic of Foote, is his insistence that politics be studied in reference to connectedness and devotion—the issue in chapter 4. Like François Truffaut, Eric Rohmer, and Paul Cox, Foote investigates political issues. But where those filmmakers tend to study intimacy in isolation and to write of intimate politics, Foote is more willing to judge the physical world against the ideals of love and community. His is a politics of intimacy.

The political contexts of his intimate dramas place Foote in the tradition of historical realism described in chapter 5. His determination to "establish a true sense of place" supports this classification, as does his desire to write the social and moral histories of coastal southeast Texas.[4] His attraction to method acting, with its emphasis on emotional authenticity, is also part of his realist impulse. But Foote's realism is not literal; it resembles Katherine Anne Porter's "real fiction," which always transforms the details of history and region into a higher order of art. Like Porter, Flannery O'Connor, and William Faulkner, Foote pursues the literary search for order and meaning within the Judeo-Christian mythos. More than his fellow southerners, however, Foote would become a healing presence in that tradition.

3. C. W. E. Bigsby, *Modern American Drama, 1945–90* (New York, 1992), 204.

4. Horton Foote, "Achieving a Sense of Place in Plays and Screenplays" (lecture at Fairleigh Dickinson College, March 30, 1987), MS in Horton Foote Papers, DeGolyer Library, Southern Methodist University, Dallas [hereinafter cited as Foote Papers].

Such artistic and religious issues are integral to *The Orphans' Home,* Foote's nine-play cycle, based on the lives of his parents, which is the subject of chapter 6. Like Foote's father, Horace Robedaux is made an orphan by the death of his father and the subsequent rejection by his new stepfather. He struggles with racism in his small town and survives World War I and the flu epidemic, also much like the author's father. But the focus of the cycle is marriage, both real and fictional, as an expression of devotion and fidelity. Horton Foote fashions this biography and coastal southeast Texas history into a story of going away from confusion and anger and coming home to love and forgiveness. By finding a wife and making a family, Horace establishes a place of order in the face of relentless change. In the process the young man finds the courage to face his past and prepare to die.

Although created under much less personal circumstances than *The Orphans' Home, Tender Mercies*—the focus of chapter 7—is also about intimacy lost and regained. Like Horace, Mac Sledge is orphaned by his loss of family, through divorce and the death of his daughter. His path to loving commitment is blocked—again as with Horace—by his anger and bitterness. In the love of Rosa Lee he finds a sense of place that connects him with family, community, and religious tradition. These connections enable him to conquer grief's temptation to turn inward. Once he admits that the female spirit has provided inspiration, Mac, like Horace, learns to share his pain and move closer to others. For him, as for all Horton Foote's characters, personal intimacy offers a means of healing.

The Young Man from Atlanta, the play for which Foote won the Pulitzer Prize for drama in 1995, at first seems different from his other plays and even screenplays. It borrows from other dramatic sources and exhibits its theatricality, foregrounding artifice like few Foote dramas. As chapter 8 demonstrates, however, Foote revises the conventions of the detective/ mystery genre in order to study intimacy issues, not aesthetic ones. In *Young Man,* mystery is embraced rather than resolved; ultimately, the uncertain and contingent nature of modern life—its essential mystery— should become, the play says, a source of empathy and compassion, not violence. While the human mind, like the writer himself, is attracted to clarity and truthfulness, it also is hungry for myth—a communal sense of imagery, language, and story that inspires kind acts and loving words.

As *The Orphans' Home, Tender Mercies,* and *The Young Man from At-*

lanta demonstrate, Horton Foote writes with the details of found art. Respecting historical fact and the raw experience of real life, he nevertheless transforms those details and facts into his personal theater of intimacy. In his dramas everyone is an orphan on an imaginary Texas landscape marked by separation and isolation. Too often his characters ignore their common reality, living as if they did not share this dark bond. Instead they build political systems that magnify the disconnection, and they deny their responsibilities to themselves and others. But the writer also imagines a loving female presence who eternally offers connection, a way home to peace and contentment. By choosing intimacy, his characters find the strength to manage fear and the courage to face the dying of the light.

2

Place and Identity

Documentary filmmaker Ross Spears believes that despite its many technical and dramatic achievements, American film generally has failed to evoke an authentic sense of place: "What American films have lacked most often are images which ring true to the poetry of real life. And real life begins with *place*."[1] Horton Foote's films are an exception to this tendency, for his plays—whether for television, theater, or cinema—respect the "poetry of real life" found in America's various places. In commissioned adaptations Foote accurately describes Harper Lee's Alabama of the depression *(To Kill a Mockingbird)* and John Steinbeck's Salinas Valley *(Of Mice and Men)*. Similarly, *Tender Mercies,* shot in Waxahachie, evokes the flat, lonely countryside of middle Texas. True to place, Foote is attentive to the details of image and speech; he respects the authenticity of American experience, particularly the South.

But the majority of his work—especially his plays—is set in one place: Wharton, Texas, his hometown. Named Richmond in some of his earliest

1. Ross Spears, "Regional Filmmaking: The James Agee Film Project," *Southern Quarterly,* XIX (Spring–Summer 1981), 223–24.

writings, but most often called Harrison, Wharton has been the primary source of his "characters, his conflicts, his language, his themes."[2] From his childhood until the present, Foote has listened to the local people, often his relatives, giving their interpretations of recent and ancient history. These stories, in their many versions, offer rich material; the tale and the teller, theme and variation form the foundation of his writing. Whether the material is sweet or critical, lyrical or cautionary, the author has always found a rich vein of storytelling in his Texas home. As Foote concludes in his preface to *Harrison, Texas,* a collection of his teleplays, his fiction comes from "the heart of the Texas Gulf Coast." The people of Wharton, Texas, are "my people. I write of them with affection, certainly, and I hope with understanding."[3]

Using Wharton as a continual source of inspiration and renewal, Horton Foote has remained faithful to coastal southeast Texas, a fidelity he demonstrates in a scene from the television drama *The Travelers* (telecast on the *Goodyear Television Playhouse* on April 27, 1952). Miss Sedora Watts and Mrs. Mayberry, two transplants from the fictional Richmond to New York City, are commiserating over Mrs. Mayberry's children. The object of their dialogue is Nadine Thornton, a visitor from Richmond who is always a good listener. The latest humiliations began, the two women say, when the children did not come for Christmas, or send cards and presents:

> *Mrs. Mayberry.* Why, I wouldn't have had any Christmas at all last year if Miss Watts hadn't remembered me with a sweet little sachet bag which she made herself.
>
> *Miss Watts.* Well, it wasn't much, honey. It was just the spirit of the thing.
>
> *Mrs. Mayberry.* But I don't bear them any malice. Do I, Miss Watts?
>
> *Miss Watts.* I'm glad to say you don't, honey.
>
> *Mrs. Mayberry.* Because that wouldn't be Christian, would it, dear?

2. Samuel Freedman, "From the Heart of Texas," *New York Times Magazine,* February 9, 1986, p. 31.

3. Horton Foote, Preface to *Harrison, Texas: Eight Television Plays by Horton Foote* (New York, 1956), viii.

Miss Watts. No, honey, it wouldn't be Christian.
Mrs. Mayberry. Always be sweet to your mother an' daddy,
dear. An' don't ever try to send them to an old peoples
home.
Nadine. No, Ma'am.[4]

Mrs. Mayberry can barely hide her bitterness behind her "sweet" words. But Miss Watts's "honey" pampers her until they seal their conspiracy with the righteous "Christian," which inspires their sermon to Nadine. In *The Travelers,* as in all Foote's personal dramas, the voices are distinctively those of coastal southeast Texas.

But as true as Foote has been to the idioms of Wharton, his own words warn that the notion of homeplaces should not be taken too literally. In an interview conducted within a year and a half of the writing of *The Travelers,* the writer explained that "every family, consciously or unconsciously, must have a spiritual and an emotional, as well as a physical, home."[5] Although his homes, like many images in individual plays, appear disarmingly specific to their region and time, Foote suggests that "emotional" and "spiritual" places—and issues—should take precedence. Studied as a whole, his writing expresses a deeply personal mythology of place in which prairies and valleys, houses and trees, rivers and birds, even the Gulf itself are not completely literal. Creatively obsessed with deprivation and healing, dislocation and identity, chaos and order, the writer transforms these concrete objects into metaphorical ones. He begins with the voices, people, and stories of Wharton, Texas, but his imagination refashions the physical landscape into symbols of the intimacy issues that haunt him.

Horton Foote's stories are versions of the essential, primitive struggle between deprivation and nurturing, objectified in the Texas landscape as the conflict between "arid . . . soil . . . almost impossible to cultivate" and fertile "river bottoms."[6] In coastal east Texas, the fields, once part of vast cotton plantations, continually recall a more orderly past when identity was easier to find and maintain. These prairies, and the ramshackle build-

---

4. Horton Foote, *The Travelers,* Act II, 23–24 (MS in Foote Papers).
5. Fredrika D. Borchard, "Horton from Wharton," *Houston Chronicle Rotogravure Magazine,* October 4, 1953, p. 7.
6. Horton Foote, *Lyndon,* Act I, 1 (MS in Foote Papers).

ings and subsistence farms around Harrison/Richmond, suggest a fall from a secure vertical world to a relative horizontal one. Sadly, but almost naturally, this dry land, an emblem of alienation, produces families broken by absent, malevolent, or self-obsessed parents. Fortunately, fertile bottoms also run through this parched ground, forming what Nadine Thornton in *The Travelers,* mimicking the Chamber of Commerce, calls "the richest cotton land . . . outside of the Nile Valley."[7] These scarce and precious valleys provide places of genuine intimacy and profound comfort. Foote's Texans inhabit a figurative landscape where forbidding, disconnected prairies meet loving, nourishing bottomlands.

As each character moves toward the time when he will assume—or deny—responsibility for his life, this imaginative landscape becomes a correlative of the journey. Some are lucky; they have already experienced the centering peace of parental love, economic security, and respect. They have been fed along the rivers. But with or without these primary attachments, at some point in their lives all Foote's characters must face the empty spaces and parched ground of neglect, loss, indifference, or death. Foote's dramas explore whether these people are able to plant roots in the river bottoms by recovering or creating loving attachments. For only by discovering the bottomland, by feeling moments of deep intimacy which can be made their own, can the characters find the courage to be themselves.

Dotting this landscape, often in clusters around the homes of rich and poor alike, are trees, revered presences in Foote's imagination. Some, like the chinaberries, are reminders of the value in the most common, simple living things. Whether chinaberry or pecan, oak or magnolia, trees reach deep into prairies, decaying plantations, and even suburban backyards, evidencing that even in the loneliest of places nourishment is possible. Children know this best; clutching the strong, supportive branches of their beloved trees, Margaret Rose, in *The Traveling Lady,* and Jem, in *To Kill a Mockingbird,* find freedom. Rooted in the assurance that they will be fed and loved, these children climb upward toward wonder and joy. Intuitively they perpetuate this sensitivity, this peace and exhilaration, by planting more trees, making more life, continuing traditions and establishing order.

As Foote's characters seek a sense of belonging on these Texas plains, they inevitably face the architecture of change. Scattered across the prai-

7. Foote, *The Travelers,* Act I, 20.

ries, but more often standing on shady streetcorners in Harrison/Richmond, are the Victorian homes built by passing generations. Large and ornate, they were constructed for affluent, burgeoning families, the aristocracy of the cotton society. When smaller farmhouses began to dot the countryside and bungalows popped up in town, these staid old structures were turned into boardinghouses. Although they are still lively and often well cared for, the shift from an elegant family home to a place where people come and go reflects the incongruous and transitory nature of twentieth-century society. Faded wallpaper is hidden behind mahogany furniture, rooms are sectioned off for tenants, and high ceilings tower above the busy pace of modern life. The inhabitants of these Victorian houses are, at best, only faintly aware of such mutation; it is their most common antagonist and sometimes their most potent ally. It is where they live.

As Foote's characters confront unsought change, these houses—whether old or new—offer a crucial sense of safety. They are the places where Jack, in his frustration with transients in *Out of My House,* claims people "can't get hurt. Haven't they found out yet? If you stay outdoors long enough, you gonna get hurt." This security of a home is the dream of Idella, the black maid in the same play: "Wants a little house of my own. Wants enough independence to tell the folks I don' lak to say [*sic*] away." Well-being, however, is never gained at the expense of others; houses need to be clean. As Robedaux says in *Out of My House,* "It is good to have a house, a car, farms . . . but it is not good if in getting those you tramp down and kill and destroy your own kind." As these examples suggest, in Foote's psychology of place, houses represent aspects of the self; Idella equates a home with personal autonomy, and Robedaux's understanding of home ownership is linked to his sense of social responsibility. Wanting a home is not unlike seeking an identity, as Sibyl explains to her boyfriend in *The Old Friends:* "I try to put this house together like I try to put my life together, and it keeps being torn apart."[8]

Although a few characters find this individuation, this proper life of their own, most live on various thresholds. Some, like Laura Lee in *Night Seasons,* are tragically paralyzed. Unable to marry or to build a house of her

8. Horton Foote, *Out of My House,* Act I, 13 (MS in Foote Papers); ibid., Act III, 7, Act IV, 19; Horton Foote, *The Old Friends,* 128 (MS in Foote Papers).

own, Laura dies, both literally and metaphorically, because she is unable to move beyond the control of her mother and cross into selfhood. Most characters, however, are like Martha Anderson and Elizabeth Vaughn, who find the courage to risk their lives. Martha, in *Flight,* impulsively marries John Dobbs, who quickly abandons her. When her family offers to take her back into the home, to offer her shelter and protection, she takes flight, leaving by train into the night. Elizabeth, whose story in *Courtship* Foote describes as "the same . . . only done differently," first follows her parents' advice to stay away from one boy, then courageously and happily chooses Horace Robedaux and a successful transition from her parents' home to her own.[9] Martha and Elizabeth seek a balance between adventure and safety; they want to cross personal thresholds that lead to new and healthy homes.

Foote's distinctive use of homes gains clarity through comparison with William Goyen, whose popular 1950s novel *The House of Breath* influenced *The Trip to Bountiful.* In his lyrical narrative Goyen writes that people "put roots" in a home "and love others there; so that whenever they left this place they would sing homesick songs about it and write poems of yearning for it, like a lover; remembering the grouping of old trees, the fall of slopes and hills, the lay of fields and the running of rivers; of animals there, and of objects lived with; of faces, and names, all of love and belonging, and forever be returning to it or leaving it again."[10] Goyen's homes, while evocative, are also literal, marked by loss and nostalgia. Foote's are not so real; they represent primary feelings of "loving and belonging" which form the basis for a healthy pattern of "returning to it or leaving it again" but are not place-specific. In Foote's imaginative world, being at home is living with security and adventure, feeling neither fused nor independent. It is not a physical place; it is the emotional and spiritual principle of being at peace living and dying.

Outside these physical and emotional homes, birds often appear as signs of a spiritual life that offers the characters, whether they believe it or not, a source of protection and courage. In *Tender Mercies,* for instance, Mac Sledge and his daughter try to remember a Christian song about a

9. Gerald C. Wood and Terry Barr, " 'A Certain Kind of Writer': An Interview with Horton Foote," *Literature / Film Quarterly,* XIV (October 1986), 235.
10. William Goyen, *The House of Breath* (New York, 1949), 41.

dove, while pictures of birds hang on the walls and real birds sing outside. More explicitly, in *The Trip to Bountiful,* Carrie Watts is driven by her need to rediscover Bountiful, a bird sanctuary. She takes strength from her belief in the God of the Ninety-first Psalm, which she quotes more completely in the play version: "He shall cover thee with His feathers and under his wing shalt thou trust: His truth shall be thy shield and buckler."[11] In *Bountiful,* as in *Tender Mercies,* birds suggest the sense of order and direction religion offers. With their appearance, there is hope that love may come to even the loneliest of people.

Water is equally powerful in Foote's religious iconography. It is most obviously present in the rivers surrounding Harrison and Richmond, where John Turner Davis *(John Turner Davis)* or Bubber Reeves *(The Chase)* feels free, where George Tyler *(Valentine's Day)* loses touch with reality, and where the Payne children *(The Habitation of Dragons)* drown. But it is not the danger in, or even the redemptive power of, the river that is dramatized in Horton Foote's writing. Foote's imagination is more captivated by the mutability of the river, which offers both the temptation of grief and the chance to heal. As Samuel Clemens explains in *The Shape of the River,* a commissioned Foote teleplay for *Playhouse 90,* the river is always changing, eternally "fooling around"—like life itself: "Everytime I get used to something, get comfortable in a way of living and I think I've learned all the things I need to know I have to start in learning all over again and figure out a new way to do and get along."[12] The river represents the inevitable struggle and loss all characters must face. The central issue of Horton Foote's theater is not the changeable nature of the river itself; it is whether an individual can "figure out a new way" by being flexible and courageous on the river.

On Foote's dry Texas land, rain is precious. But as with the rivers, rain is not merely literal; it has psychological and religious significance. In *Tomorrow* the rain reminds Fentry and Sarah of the biblical story in which Jesus walked on water. Like a mother's tears over a troubled child, rain comforts the characters as they face sickness and death. It offers them a sense of life as a mystery. Though they could never explain their emotions,

11. Horton Foote, *The Trip to Bountiful* [play] (New York, 1954), 42.
12. Horton Foote, *The Shape of the River,* Act I, 3–4 (MS in Fred Coe Collection, University of Wisconsin, Madison).

the two are groping toward a unique sense of miracle. They can no longer expect Jesus to appear, but the love they share is redemptive in its own way. The rain inspires a profound intimacy that offers hope; it comforts and heals them.

Although seldom explicitly visible, the waters of the Gulf of Mexico provide an even more powerful source of healing. In *The Trip to Bountiful* Carrie Watts, during the bus ride to Harrison, tells her new friend about the value of the Gulf for Ludie and her: "He [Ludie] wasn't nervous back in Bountiful. Neither was I. The breeze from the Gulf would always quiet your nerves. You could sit on your front gallery and smell the ocean blowing in around you."[13] The sweetness of this unusually lyrical passage derives from Carrie's selective memory and nostalgia for the natural world, but her mind and spirit are the real subjects of her words. With a sense of connection to a primary rhythm of life, Ludie and Carrie feel a peace which comes from the spirit of love, embodied in the distant but powerful presence of the Gulf, lying just beyond the view of Ludie, Carrie, and the others.

In an early draft of *Tender Mercies* Foote once again uses birds and water to suggest the presence of an unrealized spiritual ideal. Near the story's end, Mac and Sonny throw a football as Rosa Lee sings "On the wings of a snow white dove, / He sends his pure, sweet love. / A sign from above. / On the wings of a dove." Madonna-like, she watches approvingly and lovingly as the birds return to the water. In Horton Foote's words, "MAC and SONNY continue playing football. ROSA LEE watches as overhead, high above, geese can be seen flying on their way to the gulf."[14] For a brief moment, without their full knowledge, the characters gain the rest and contentment that are at the heart of Foote's religious vision. Under the wings and refreshed by the water, Mac, Rosa Lee, and Sonny are home.

Implicit in Foote's personal use of Texas landscape is his vision of American history, especially its tendency toward rootlessness. According to Foote, twentieth-century anxiety results from the physical and emotional dislocation produced by modern American life. For example, farmers who live close to the earth and believe in the nurturing power of nature

---

13. Foote, *Bountiful*, 44.
14. Horton Foote, *Tender Mercies* [screenplay] (MS in Foote Papers), 108.

are newly tempted to exploit the land for profit. Small-town businesses are undermined when residents depart for cities; their flight leaves families separated and often broken. Work is only for profit and expresses little communal spirit. While many characters consider God either irrelevant or terribly distant, even believers find themselves confused by or afraid of a God of guilt and retribution. The centers which brought people together no longer hold.

Because of this epidemic of dislocation, finding a place becomes a pressing concern, and a central metaphor, in Foote's writing. Understood metaphorically, having a place is not the same as staying put, either physically or emotionally, according to the writer. He satirizes characters who are provincial or inflexible, and he is not sentimental about small towns or the old days. In fact, going away is often a necessity in his plays, and freedom is a goal for all his strongest characters. The specter that haunts his imaginative landscape is not Houston, the Astrodome, suburbia, or shopping malls, but isolation—the absence of intimacy. And his prescription is not a return to the land or villages; it is connection to loved ones and a community—natural, professional, or religious.

Consequently place is synonymous with establishing an identity based on a creative use of the past. Foote rejects the radical individualism of west Texas, seeing only loneliness in the worship of solitude and willfulness. As an east Texas writer, a neighbor to the Deep South, Foote finds identity in relationships, in knowing one's place. That is why he is respectful of an aristocracy which at every turn he recognizes as racist and sexist. Despite the horrors and injustice found in plantation society, it offered ties of kinship which unified the living and the dead; identity came with the territory. The strict responsibilities and demands of convention, though often stifling and even violent, might neutralize the alienating forces in the new commercial, fluid America.

Emblematic of history serving personhood are Horace Robedaux's efforts, in *Roots in a Parched Ground,* to place a tombstone on his father's grave. The young orphan tries to orient himself, to establish a sense of self, by publicly marking his father's life. But he receives confusing information about which grave is the correct one; an older woman names one place, and a black caretaker chooses another. For a Horton Foote character, identity may never be fully realized in time, but life is made valuable and humane by the desire for roots and wings. With both sadness and humor,

Foote's people—like Horace Robedaux—long for true bearings, ways to map their lives and note their passing. Searching for a place on the Texas landscape in Horton Foote's plays represents the eternal quest for identity.

Similarly, Foote observes, writing serves his need to put his personal tombstones in their proper places. In a revealing 1986 interview for the *New York Times,* he explained: "No matter how far away I've been—New York, London, Hollywood—half of me is always thinking about Wharton, trying to figure out some aspect of this life back here."[15] Writing is a form of meditation on his past, a means of creating a version of life in Wharton that will empower his present. Foote's work helps him to make Wharton's history his own, investing it with meaning that can awaken courage. Writing reduces the confusion of the past, controls fear, and nurtures choices. In the creative act of storytelling, Foote finds a healthy intimacy which frees him to go home to his past and then leave it again—in pursuit of order and courage.

In a public place like the theater, representing intimacy is a problematic and complex task. For Foote, the heart of this matter is pinpointed by Ortega y Gasset, whose essays on modernism, especially "The Dehumanization of Art," describe how the irony and formalism of contemporary art is considered a new elitism. According to Ortega y Gasset, the self-referential, socially irresponsible, and primitively playful side of the cult of the artist requires a sensibility not available to most viewers and audiences. In both drama and film such modernism destroys the traditional sense of sacred space in the theater. The author no longer needs to imagine a world familiar to the audience. Sincerity and sympathy—expressions of intimacy between actor and observer—are not necessary or desired.[16]

Not wanting to align himself with the centrifugal forces contributing to this brokenness and fragmentation, Foote pursues a theater vitalized by its return to what Ortega y Gasset calls " 'lived' reality." In this theater the playwright seeks to recover the primary connection between "the majority of people" and the illusion of "real life": "A man likes a play when he has become interested in the human destinies presented to him, when the love and hatred, the joys and sorrows of the personages so move his heart that

15. Freedman, "From the Heart of Texas," 61.
16. José Ortega y Gasset, "The Dehumanization of Art," in *The Dehumanization of Art and Other Essays on Art, Culture, and Literature* (Princeton, 1968), 1–54.

he participates in it all as though it were happening in real life." From this premodern premise—with its real-life norm—Foote fashions a theater so stubborn in its avoidance of cliche, formula, and melodrama that it continually risks dedramatizing itself into antitheater. It invites repetition and encourages boredom, if necessary, in order to test the line between fiction and reality. An essentially transparent drama, it prefers life to artifice, even when that preference challenges the structure and usual standards of theater and film.[17]

Because of this hyperrealism, Horton Foote's work is not as mainstream as it might at first appear. On the one hand, his naturalistic characters and preference for linear, historical plots easily associate him with the traditional theater defined by Robert Brustein in *Reimagining American Theatre:* "More often than not, American mainstream drama continues to explore the causes behind the effects; the event to be excavated is still the guilt of the (generally older generation) protagonists; and the drama retains the air of a courtroom, complete with investigations, indictments, arraignments, condemnations, and punishments." But Foote's work in both theater and film is more static and less "Newtonian" than it appears. Although he uses political and psychological themes in his plays, Foote freezes those issues in time, preferring a personal exploration of the connection between intimacy and courage. In the process, Foote's "suspicion of art" becomes most contemporary.[18] His humanism transforms traditional dramatic realism into a strange, often dark world where closure is realized only in death.

Horton Foote believes in what he calls a "basic truth" of creation: "a man writes better about the places and the people he knows and understands." His place is Texas, specifically coastal southeast Texas, which he says "has always seemed to me to be the land of drama." As a playwright, he stays close to what Stark Young describes as the "alive, unself-conscious and rural" speech of Texas' "plain people . . . plain towns and circumstances."[19] This Texas idiom is Horton Foote's contribution to the history

17. Ibid., 18, 8; José Ortega y Gasset, "The Idea of Theater," in *Phenomenology and Art* (New York, 1975), 178.

18. Robert Brustein, *Reimagining American Theatre* (New York, 1991), 25, 24. See also Bigsby, *Modern American Drama,* 10.

19. Borchard, "Horton from Wharton," 6; Stark Young, Foreword to Horton Foote, *The Traveling Lady* (New York, 1955), 6.

of American place-writing. As a screenwriter, he translates this style into film and answers Ross Spears's call for movies based on the "poetry of real life."

Like the best regional writers, Foote fashions local materials into a fictional and personal place. Shaped by his imagination, the Texas landscape dramatizes the eternal pursuit of identity that energizes Foote's writing. By continually reinventing life in Wharton, Foote creates his own story of the area and its past. Though his is only one version, one truth among many, the process offers the author a degree of peace and order. Not unlike what happens with his characters, Foote's sense of self begins and ends with loving attachments to family, land, community, or religion. For humans real and fictional, the road to peace and contentment is unimaginable without this intimacy, without an emotional and spiritual home. While Foote recognizes that the rootless, mythless life of contemporary America makes personhood especially elusive, he believes the search for authentic love is a primal need. Given these conditions, theater best serves its artists and audiences, according to Foote, when it is designed to keep art human.[20]

20. See also the memorial pamphlet to Herbert Berghof, where (p. 35) Foote quotes Pablo Neruda: "Though human values are endangered, we can keep a theatre alive which without distortion is simple, critical, but not inhuman; which moves forward like a river, bounded only by the banks of its own making" (MS in Foote Papers).

3

Belief, Courage, and the Female Spirit

In *Tender Mercies,* the 1983 film for which Horton Foote received an Academy Award for best original screenplay, Mac Sledge, an aging country and western singer, is fighting a long struggle with alcoholism. He is fortunate enough to stumble across Rosa Lee, the owner of a small old roadside motel, the Mariposa. With her support he is able to climb out of his self-destructive depressions. He begins by working at the motel, marries Rosa Lee, and slowly learns to be close to her child, Sonny. But even as he recovers, temptation refuses to disappear. Late one afternoon, despite his wife's willingness to sit nearby and listen to his latest songs, Mac is overcome by restlessness and disconnection. He hurries out of the motel, declaring, "Now, don't feel sorry for me, Rosa Lee. I'm not dead, you know."[1]

A sequence follows in which Mac drives recklessly through the Texas countryside, almost provokes a fight in a small cafe, buys liquor, and narrowly misses getting into a collision at an intersection. Meanwhile, Rosa Lee and Sonny try to distract themselves. Rosa Lee listens for Mac, repeat-

---

1. Horton Foote, *Three Screenplays: "To Kill a Mockingbird," "Tender Mercies," and "The Trip to Bountiful"* (New York, 1989) [hereinafter cited as *Three Screenplays*], 113.

edly looks out the window, and walks to the highway to bleed off some anxiety. But the conversation between mother and son produces more agitation than comfort, for it keeps returning to thoughts of violence (Sonny's father's death in Vietnam) and addiction (drugs at school). Mac's destructive attachment to alcohol haunts his wife and her child all the more in his absence. Finally, Rosa Lee ends her vigil and goes to bed.

Rosa Lee is a believer, a good Baptist raised in the local church. She has strong roots in her town; in her family, church, and community she has a sense of belonging that is included in her tradition of a humble, prayerful, religious life. With Mac out in the night and Sonny asleep, Rosa Lee lies in bed and prays, "Show me Thy way, O Lord, and teach me Thy path. Lead me in Thy truth and teach me. For Thou art the God of my salvation. On Thee do I wait all the day." As she speaks these words, Mac returns in his truck. Rosa Lee breaks off her prayer in order to greet him and offer "a little soup."[2]

This sequence raises important questions regarding the religious nature of Horton Foote's work. Should Mac's return be interpreted as an answer to Rosa Lee's prayer? Is the Providence that is so integral to Rosa Lee's experience also part of the vision of the screenwriter? Or could it have been added by Bruce Beresford, the director of *Tender Mercies?* In other words, is there an identification of providential order and dramatic structure in this film? And finally, are basic religious issues specific to this story, or do they inform all of Horton Foote's work? Put simply: what is the writer's religious vision, if any, as expressed in his work?

Such questions led me to ask the writer, during an interview in July of 1985, to describe his religious background and beliefs. At that time—and for a number of interviewers since—he nicely sidestepped the question, although his words are a good place to start: "Well, I don't really like to. I am very religious, but really don't like to get into that because it would give you the wrong idea. I don't ever really write from that point of view. I say I am religious because I am deeply religious. Yes, I am. But, um, it would never occur to me to proselytize. And it must be more deeply rooted in my make-up than I realize."[3] Though Foote defines himself as a very religious man, he does not want to be accused of proselytizing and never writes to justify his own perspective.

2. Ibid., 119.
3. Wood and Barr, " 'Certain Kind of Writer,' " 231.

And he is clearly right about the absence of a consistent, overt emphasis on religion in his plays. Few of Horton Foote's stories, whether staged or filmed, are concerned with religious people, words, or rituals. Carrie Watts *(The Trip to Bountiful)* and Rosa Lee *(Tender Mercies)* are in a minority in his work. He has written about a minister in crisis *(Ludie Brooks)* and the devolution of religious experience *(The Land of the Astronauts),* but those plays are exceptions. And even when Foote creates religious characters, they are full of doubt, indecision, guilt, and anxiety, just like the nonbelievers. Carrie Watts, for instance, is a deeply religious woman who takes strength from the "blessed assurance" that the Lord will lead her home. Nevertheless, feelings of loss, remorse, and even self-obsession, accompany her when she returns to Bountiful. Occasionally narcissism overwhelms believers; a woman on her balcony in *1918* and Dixie in *Tender Mercies* react to death by declaring that God has singled them out for misfortune. Many of Foote's believers are quick to judge others and fail in their ministry to the weak and needy *(A Nightingale).* Some even display their religion as if it were the latest fashion, like a trendy lifestyle, at once superficial and dehumanizing *(The Land of the Astronauts).*

Consequently, any understanding of religious context in Foote's dramas begins not with simple affirmations but with dark truths. Although he never explains the differences between people, time and again Foote returns to the essential inequities in the human condition. Men (and women) are not, in his view, created equal; their gifts are distributed with an almost genetic finality. Sadder yet, each person's condition is irreversible, and personal struggles, once they surface, remain as eternal conflicts and challenges. Individuals can act lovingly toward each other, they can honor and protect their fellow man, but no one is saved in any definitive way. No clear means of transformation and no quick fixes exist in Foote's imaginative world. All his people share a common need for security and love, but they never fully triumph over their own pasts or personalities. They find peace and contentment, first, by accepting and accommodating to their personal history, with all its limitations and obligations, and second, by acknowledging the inevitability of death.

Redemption in Foote's world is thus a matter of connection and adjustment rather than transcendence. No one escapes from the cycle of birth and death; in fact, that cycle furnishes a central reality for Foote. His best characters do not demand power, truth, or even joy from life; rather, they recognize that seemingly innumerable forces are beyond their control. They find their most satisfying peace when they stop railing against divine authority and the injustices of the material world; freedom becomes possible when they quit bargaining with fate. Most happily, a sense of community emerges from this compromise with the forces of life, one that nourishes the alienated, lonely individual in life and in death.

Central to this theater of intimacy—and the sense of community it imagines—is the presence of saintlike women in Foote's work. While Foote dramatizes the obstacles to female power and freedom, his ideal women do not necessarily demand social action. They may, like Sarah Nancy in *Blind Date,* push beyond the simple pieties of traditional roles for females, struggling to free themselves from submission, or like Rosa Lee in *Tender Mercies,* they also may be wives, mothers, and homemakers. It is not women's social position or habits that intrigue Foote; it is their deep connection to the life process. For example, he says that the woman in *Old Man,* his 1960 adaption of a Faulkner story for television, "was always (and remains so) a delight to me" because of her "acceptance of everything that happened. Always finding something in the journey itself to enjoy in spite of cold, hunger, childbirth under the most horrifying conditions, infestation of snakes, and gunfire." Foote admires women who refuse to fight against life's inevitable pain, disappointment, and failure. Their radical acceptance of the human condition allows them to celebrate "the journey itself"—without regret, guilt, or even complaints.[4]

With this acceptance comes the ability to discriminate and focus on life's essentials. This perspective is what distinguishes Rosa Lee in *Tender Mercies,* according to the author: "Mac Sledge will have dark periods for the rest of his life—doubts and confusion. It isn't that Rosa Lee doesn't have them. But she has a purer sense of what it's all about. . . . She has her own confusion, like the death of her husband. But she doesn't really doubt what she thinks is the final thrust of things."[5] The strength of Foote's powerful women comes from their closeness to the primary patterns of life.

4. Horton Foote, "On First Dramatizing Faulkner," in *Faulkner, Modernism, and Film: Faulkner and Yoknapatawpha, 1978,* ed. Evans Harrington and Ann J. Abadie (Jackson, Miss., 1979), 54. See Daniel C. Maguire's "The Feminization of God and Ethics," *Christianity and Crisis,* XLII (March 15, 1982), 59–67, which is remarkably close to Foote in emphasizing the role of affect, nurturing, and intimacy in healthy and peaceful living.

5. Horton Foote, interview with author, October 24, 1985.

Whatever the style of their lives, they are inspired by their attachments—to others (like Rosa Lee), to the rituals of daily living (like Mrs. Thornton in *The Oil Well*), and to the cycles of nature (like Carrie Watts in *The Trip to Bountiful*). Women have powers of intimacy often ignored by men in their race for power and control.

In Foote's imagination these madonna-like women become emblems of religion as a source of order. In the twentieth century, as more and more people drift through aimless, rootless lives, their need to draw strength from a grounding principle, a basic mythology, becomes critically important. Foote maintains that, in the South, Protestantism often provides such a foundation: "I think there's a lot of strength in the Protestant tradition—both for Blacks and Whites. I think it's been something that's helped them to bring order into their lives. . . . And I certainly know that it is a strength for many, many people." But it is not only southern Protestantism that impresses Foote. It is the power of belief—no matter the system—to uphold people in the face of adversity. In an interview for *Christianity Today* he explained, "You know, a lot of difficulty comes to people in their lives, and you have to ask yourself, What gets them through it? And if you are at all honest, you have to say that you may or may not understand it, but you have to witness to the fact that their religion must sustain them a great deal."[6]

Religion, then, helps to lay the foundation upon which is constructed Foote's most cherished emotion—courage. Ironically, by giving themselves to living orders, his characters—inspired by the focused, discriminating love of certain women—gain an identity, a precious experience for modern men. By knowing themselves and committing to things they believe, his people discover the courage to face life's "impossible things": "I'm always amazed at the grace of people, how they take adversity, how they face afflictions and addictions, how they manage to meet impossible things. If you have to say there is a theme to my work, it's this theme of people's courage."[7] This courage to be oneself, a courage born from beliefs and the attachments they foster, is the source of all valuable freedom in Foote's imaginative world. With courage comes the power of choice, the

6. Ibid.; David Neff, "Going Home to the Hidden God," *Christianity Today,* April 4, 1986, p. 30.
7. Samir Hachem, "Foote-Work," *Horizon,* XXIX (April 1986), 40.

flexibility to change, the passion to live, and the strength to face death. Graced by courage, his character's lives become their own.

Not only does the female spirit offer order and courage; she embraces mystery as well. Her acceptance of life and intimacy—and of the uncertainties inherent in both—frees her to experience mystery as a form of realism and wisdom, a point Foote makes explicit in his interview with *Post Script:* "Well, I think, my God, how can you say it's not a mystery? You never know what the next day is going to bring and you just sit and wait and you do the best you can with what's there. . . . I think it is essentially naive to think that you can really control life because you can't."[8] Otherwise recalcitrant and threatening, life experienced as mystery becomes wonderful. With a less clear destination, the journey becomes everything and all life sacred, according to Foote's female principle.

Most reassuring is how a special woman's selflessness intimates a divine spirit of love that nurtures all life. God is first imagined in Foote's work as powerful, just, and the source of a great healing order. And he is male, a father. But he is also distant, and the time of his miracles, of a blessed assurance, is past. The magical calming presence of God can only be realized in the fallen, confusing present, which is the province of the female. In Foote's vision, authentic peace is realized in the return to the absent father. But the courage to find that spiritual peace can only be found under the care of women. Though the process remains incomplete and peace is never fully realized, the saintly presence of exemplary women, and the spirit they embody, leads the way home.

Foote's vision of the female spirit has interesting analogs in psychology and philosophy. Carl Jung and Paul Tillich, for example, critique the twentieth century's failure to integrate female qualities, as traditionally defined, into individuals and society. Believing this imbalance an essential weakness in the modern temper, Erik Erikson imagines in *Identity: Youth and Crisis* that social conditions can be ameliorated by the extension of women's private virtue into the public arena:

Maybe if women would only gain the determination to represent publicly what they have always stood for privately in evolution and in history (realism in householding, responsibility of upbringing,

8. Wood, "Horton Foote: An Interview," 10.

resourcefulness in peacekeeping, and devotion to healing), they might well add an ethically restraining, because truly supranational, power to politics in the widest sense.[9]

Similar to Foote in their call to caretaking and healing, these writers nevertheless are more politicized and futuristic than the Texas dramatist. He might agree with them but could not be their disciple.

The most useful context for understanding Foote's representation of the feminine—and the most immediate and powerful influence in his life—is the Christian Science Church. Although members of his family have followed a number of religious denominations, including the Episcopal and Methodist Churches, Horton Foote's mother became a Christian Scientist. The writer followed her into that faith and has practiced it throughout his adult life. Although Foote says he does not write from "that point of view," the writings of Mary Baker Eddy (the denomination's founder) and other Christian Scientists influence the ethos of his dramas, especially his views of sexuality, women, and religion.[10]

Since Christian Science begins with the recognition that God is a unifying, transcendent figure defined by divine otherness, sexuality does not at first seem relevant. As Robert Peel explains in a recent study of the religion, Christian Scientists do not worship "a bisexual or androgynous God. . . . The fact is that the very concept of sex is outside the Christian Science understanding of Deity. Sex belongs wholly to the finite human sense of being, with its endless dualisms of night and day, cold and hot, up and

9. Erik Erikson, *Identity: Youth and Crisis* (New York, 1968), 262. The anthology *Religion and Sexism: Images of Woman in the Jewish and Christian Traditions,* ed. Rosemary Radford Ruether (New York, 1974), includes two essays which place the work of Tillich and Erikson in a feminist context: Patricia Martin Doyle, "Women and Religion: Psychological and Cultural Implications," 15–40, and Joan Arnold Romero, "The Protestant Principle: A Woman's-Eye View of Barth and Tillich," 319–40.

10. Because the life and work of Mary Baker Eddy are so controversial, there are few balanced interpretations. Useful studies include Barbara Brown Zikmund, "The Feminist Thrust of Sectarian Christianity," in *Women of Spirit: Female Leadership in the Jewish and Christian Traditions,* ed. Rosemary Ruether and Eleanor McLaughlin (New York, 1979), 205–24, and esp. Stephen Gottschalk, *The Emergence of Christian Science in American Religious Life* (Berkeley, 1973). See also Robert Peel's three-volume life: *Mary Baker Eddy: The Years of Discovery* (New York, 1966), *Mary Baker Eddy: The Years of Trial* (New York, 1971), and *Mary Baker Eddy: The Years of Authority* (New York, 1977).

down, mind and matter, life and death. Even if one sees any of these pairs as indicating a continuum rather than a rigid polarity, they remain outside the undivided oneness of God—mere benchmarks of finitude." Sex is an expression of divided, finite man, not the divine spirit. Or, as Mary Baker Eddy expressed it concisely in *Science and Health,* "Gender . . . is a quality, not of God, but a characteristic of mortal mind."[11]

Nevertheless, human beings live in the finite world and thus must use the images and language of sexuality. And so, while God remains essentially mysterious, it is proper to use the language of androgyny because, as Mary Baker Eddy says, God unites the "creation . . . intelligence, and . . . Truth" of the "ideal man" with the "life and . . . Love" of the "ideal woman." Consequently, those who would pattern their lives on divine example must embrace both genders, integrating qualities of the opposite sex into oneself. In Christian Science, as in Foote's writing, "one's true spiritual identity . . . embraces all . . . that human beings may think of as masculine or feminine."[12]

In order to create a psychological and spiritual androgyny and redress the historical dominance of the masculine in society and religion, the feminine needs to be recovered. Again the key is found in the writings of Mary Baker Eddy, who in a provocative passage from *Science and Health* asserts that the Virgin Mary "conceived" not just the historical Jesus but the idea of God as spiritual love. From this source love becomes a potent force against fear, its eternal antagonist; in Eddy's words, "divine Love . . . casteth out fear" and makes "Moral courage" possible. Without speculating on the ultimate nature of God, the founder of Christian Science finally tips the scales on the side of the female spirit: "In divine Science, we have not as much authority for considering God masculine, as we have for considering Him feminine, for Love imparts the clearest idea of Deity." Belief in an immanent God—imagined as a female in love with life—is the ultimate source of courage, where, according to Horton Foote and Christian Science, all responsible life begins and ends.[13]

11. Robert Peel, *Health and Medicine in the Christian Tradition* (New York, 1988), 33, and Mary Baker Eddy, *Science and Health with Key to the Scriptures* (Boston, 1934), 305.

12. Eddy, *Science and Health,* 517; Peel, *Health and Medicine,* 41.

13. Gottschalk, *Emergence of Christian Science,* 52–53; Eddy, *Science and Health,* 29, 180, 327, 517. The female image of God is a timely and provocative subject. Most influential has been the work of Rosemary Radford Ruether, esp. *Mary—The Feminine Face of the*

In her search for a theodicy free from the vindictiveness of Calvinism, Mary Baker Eddy envisioned a "wholly good" God radically committed to freedom, individuation, and life without evil. As Stephen Gottschalk has summarized in his seminal work on the place of Christian Science in American religious experience, her "real theological motive was linked to the rigorous Augustinian and Puritan defense of God's absolute sovereignty and goodness which refuses to ascribe evil in any form to a God who is wholly good. The iron logic which led Calvin from the passionate insistence upon God's sovereignty to the 'horrible' doctrine of predestination led her to the very opposite conclusion: that God's infinite goodness precluded evil from being anything other than the temporary effect of the failure to apprehend His reality in its fullness."[14] Such a purely nurturant, loving God—with powerful female qualities—is implied in the work of Horton Foote. This God may not give providential order to the Foote characters who do not desire his presence. Nevertheless, this God of Christian Science exists in the subtext of Foote's writing as the standard for judging action in the text itself.

For example, two of Foote's works, both written from a woman's point of view, are structured by the primal need to return to such a father/mother God. One is the screenplay for *To Kill a Mockingbird,* in which Foote emphasizes that Harper Lee's novel is a memory play. In recounting her childhood experiences of sexism and racism in a small town, Scout remembers her victory over fear, using the words of her youth to recover the courage she discovered back then. Just before she completes her tale, the mature Scout assures herself that the foundation for her strength was Atticus, a male father and God. Despite Jem's doubts, the indifference of the townspeople, and Scout's own ignorance and confusion, Atticus was

---

Church (Philadelphia, 1977) and *Sexism and God-Talk: Toward a Feminist Theology* (Boston, 1983). See also Andrew M. Greeley, *The Mary Myth: On the Femininity of God* (New York, 1977); Joan Chamberlain Engelsman, *The Feminine Dimension of the Divine* (Philadelphia, 1979); Virginia Ramey Mollenkott, *The Divine Feminine: The Biblical Imagery of God as Female* (New York, 1983); and Elizabeth A. Johnson, *She Who Is: The Mystery of God in Feminist Theological Discourse* (New York, 1992). Closest to the vision articulated in the writing of Horton Foote is Patricia Wilson-Kastner, *Faith, Feminism, and the Christ* (Philadelphia, 1983), esp. chap. 5 ("Who Is This Christ?"), 89–119.

14. Stephen Gottschalk, "Theodicy after Auschwitz and the Reality of God," *Union Seminary Quarterly Review,* XLI (1987), 84.

an omnipresent father: "Atticus. He would be in Jem's room all night. And he would be there when Jem waked up in the morning."[15] Complete faith in such a father as a divine presence, Scout implies, gave her the courage she needed in her youth and will regain as an adult.

The other story is *The Trip to Bountiful*. Typical of Foote's method of writing with theme and variation, *Bountiful* complements *Mockingbird*, offering a similar return, but this time to a mother God. As Carrie Watts remembers it, Bountiful is a woman's world, a fertile land for Carrie and her friend Callie Davis. In Carrie's homeplace, she says to Thelma, "You just had to drop seeds in the ground and the crops would spring up." Not transcendent and majestic like Atticus's world, Bountiful is full of sacred time and relationships. It is more than people, according to Carrie; it brings about eternal peace of connectedness, the joy of female intimacy: "The fields, the trees, and the smell of the Gulf. I always got my strength from that. Not from houses, not from people. It's so quiet. So eternally quiet. I'd forgotten the peace and the quiet."[16] Just as Scout is inspired by the memory of Atticus, Carrie is strengthened by her love for Bountiful, a continually nurturing female place—and God.

This love of women is both personal and literal for Foote. Raised by grandmothers, aunts, and a most devoted mother, the writer naturally reciprocated with deep respect, first for them and later for his wife and daughters. *Tender Mercies* can therefore be seen from a biographical point of view, as a love poem for Lillian Vallish Foote. Through the character of Rosa Lee, Foote testifies to his wife's ability to be an emotionally authentic

15. Foote, *Three Screenplays*, 80. Throughout his career Foote has been careful with adaptation. Only the repeated insistence of his wife and the encouragement of Harper Lee convinced the reluctant writer that he should tackle *To Kill a Mockingbird*. His reservations increased when Hollywood pressured him throughout the 1960s to continue translating other southern authors to the screen. Always wanting to write in his own voice, Foote has preferred works that offer chances for self-expression. In *Tomorrow*, for example, the central character Sarah Eubanks and all the details of her relationship with Fentry are Foote's creations. As Rebecca Briley has summarized, "Although Foote prefers personal writing, his success in adapting these writers relies on his recognition of similar regional accents. And then, like the writers themselves, he transforms those place-specific stories into universal experiences of love, loss, and reconciliation." Rebecca Briley, "Southern Accents," in *Horton Foote: A Casebook,* ed. Gerald C. Wood (New York, 1998), 50. In each case where Foote's version reiterates the original, I have compared the texts and used only material congenial to his vision.

16. Foote, *Three Screenplays*, 184, 213.

person—to have her own anxieties and doubts—while remaining empathetic and loving. As Hallie Foote, the writer's older daughter, explains, "There's a kind of woman my father always writes—gentle but very strong. . . . Often, they seem dependent on the man, but they exhibit this strength. These women survive and they do it with dignity. Rosa Lee in 'Tender Mercies' is sort of fearless. She could allay the fears in Mac. And that's how my mother is. She believes so completely in my father and his talent. It's almost like she had a plan for him."[17]

Horton Foote's drama, while often biographical, always moves beyond the merely personal. He feels that women, although pursued by the same demons known to men, are generally better at loving, in part because of their acute interest in the lives of others. Like the African American characters in Foote's works, the women of Richmond/Harrison, Texas, have a much greater sense of and regard for emotional attachment. Women are also better able to describe the intentions of others, especially men, who are largely oblivious to these dramas, or at least unable to articulate them with the complexity they deserve. That women occasionally pay a price for such impulses is reflected in Foote's analysis of a dying patriarchy.

These gender issues do not remain historical and political; in the subtext of Horton Foote's writing they become integral to his personal, primarily mental, theater. The women he finds most delightful are those who appeal to his imagination by embodying a graceful spirit desperately needed in contemporary life. The feeling of bonding that humanizes people, that gives them a place, a proper relation to the world, is the feminine imperative in Foote's universe. Without it, men and women alike are victims, and sometimes even agents, of disorder, absurdity, and death. But the feminine impulse—whether in males or females—is the eternal desire for life, continuity, identity, and meaning in the face of a very real darkness. In the name of this female spirit Foote critiques the Calvinistic view of God as wrathful and vindictive, exploring instead God's eternal goodness. In the process Foote accepts the traditional view that, from humanity's limited perspective, God appears masculine and distant. At the same time, however, Foote's saintlike women are so powerfully close to existential realities that they challenge the patriarchal God, even in the person of the historical Jesus, for influence and efficacy.

17. Freedman, "From the Heart of Texas," 62.

While references to religion are only scattered throughout Foote's works, there is a Christian context for his theater of intimacy. His believers are as susceptible to obsession and viciousness as his nonbelievers. Even the most pious characters must face grief, despair, and death. But the imagery and stories of Christianity, as refracted through the lens of the Christian Science tradition, inform the subtext of his work. In Foote's plays, whether for the stage or film, genuine belief brings peace and order. Few of his characters recognize its efficacy, choose its power, but it has a living presence nevertheless. In Foote's imagination, love is a female spirit offering hope and courage.

4

The Politics of Intimacy

Harvey Weems . . . for all his good looks and his money, he was the loneliest person alive.
—*The Midnight Caller*

Fascism is in the heart.
—*People in the Show*

In the *New York Times Magazine* for February 9, 1986, Horton Foote explained that his social views are not designed to foment change: "I have social points of view that are not shared by a lot of people [in Wharton], but I never picked fights much. I listened to them and tried to understand what made them feel the way they did. Not that I've even understood, but I've learned to listen. I'm a social writer in the sense that I want to record, but not in the sense of trying to change people's minds."[1] Foote is a "social writer," he says, because he is very attentive to social and historical realities. He tries to record accurately the pressures and joys that come from

1. Freedman, "From the Heart of Texas," 61.

living in a community like Wharton, but he has no personal agenda for social change, no intention of modifying the behavior of people back home or even their points of view.

Although Foote's words are accurate and helpful, they raise more questions than they answer. Are these modifications needed only in Wharton, Texas? Or, if they reflect Foote's social conscience and approach to writing, what is the writer's attitude toward the political views of his audiences and of society in general? Is he indifferent, or does he have a political position not expressed in his writing? In any case, where do readers and audiences find norms for evaluating the social actions of his characters? In other words, what psychological and religious standards, if any, are implied when he claims to "record," not "change," the points of view he dramatizes?

The political material in his work suggests that Foote is neither reactionary nor apolitical, for power is irresponsibly exercised by wealthy against poor, young against old, aristocrats against immigrants, even the beautiful against the less attractive. But the most intrusive and debilitating social evils are racism and sexism. In Foote's plays African Americans continue to suffer from institutionalized violence. Most obviously, in *Convicts,* the prisoners are African American males, the word *convict* signifying the brutal social realities faced by people of color. Like African American men, women of every color carry special burdens under the rigid patriarchal system Foote analyzes. In *Tears of My Sister,* a teleplay for *Gulf Playhouse* in August of 1953, the camera assumes the point of view of Cecilia Monroe, who is anticipating the marriage of her older sister, Bessie. During the play Cecilia is slowly introduced to the reason for Bessie's repeated tearful episodes. Since the death of their father, Bessie has felt the pressure to marry an older, wealthy man, not the man she loves. Bessie slides toward this conclusion because she, like her mother and sister, feels powerless to make choices and change her life. Worse than this paralysis is the inauthenticity the women feel as the objects of male fantasies. Although Cecilia fights the loss of her innocence, she explains: "Mama says men understand not a thing about the sorrows of women. She says it just scares them. She says all men want women to be regular doll babies all the time. Happy and good-natured and with no troubles."[2] Unable to share these dark feelings

2. Horton Foote, *Selected One-Act Plays of Horton Foote,* ed. Gerald C. Wood (Dallas, 1989) [hereinafter cited as *Selected One-Acts*], 161.

of confusion and powerlessness with men, women are condemned to an emotional, and often a financial, poverty. In Horton Foote's theater, such inauthenticity is horrifying.

Equally debilitating are the social expectations which make establishing an identity so difficult for women. In *Blind Date,* another one-act play (first produced at the Loft Studio in Los Angeles in 1982), the main character is Sarah Nancy, a young woman who rebels against traditional expectations for her gender. As she prepares for a date, her aunt Dolores reminds her that girls need to be "peppy" and "gracious" at all times. But Sarah Nancy ignores the advice and instead responds sarcastically to her date, Felix Robertson. When he tries to sing, Sarah declares, "If you can sing, a screech owl can sing . . . I'd rather listen to a jackass bray than you sing. You look like a warthog and you bray like a jackass."[3] Significantly, Felix accepts this brashness, and the subsequent leveling that occurs between the two young people becomes the basis of their growing friendship. Only with genuine emotion, even if that includes destroying old gender roles, can women realize a sense of identity and intimacy.

A most helpful play for discovering Horton Foote's approach to certain injustices is *Only the Heart,* written in 1943 and the only Foote play to reach Broadway until *The Young Man from Atlanta* in 1997. This three-act studies Mamie Borden's attempts to give direction to her daughter, Julia, who has just completed high school and is considering marrying her boyfriend, Albert. An attractive and energetic person, Mamie Borden feels that she knows what is best for Julia; the mother therefore encourages her only child to skip college and marry Albert because Mamie secretly fears the girl will pursue Less Roberts, an unacceptable suitor. Mamie uses Julia's fear of rejection and lost opportunity to manipulate her into accepting Albert's proposal, which has also been engineered by Mamie. The mother also hides knowledge of Mr. Borden's continuing affair with a Bohemian woman.

After Julia and Albert get married, Mamie lures her son-in-law into her business activities, partly as a substitute for her absent husband. As Albert becomes work-obsessed and Julia more lonely, her aunt, India Hamilton, fears Less Roberts's return to Richmond will lead Julia into infidelity. Albert spends more time with Mamie than with Julia, and when the daughter

3. Ibid., 386.

begins seeing Less again, she becomes the subject of gossip in the small town. Although their meetings are innocent, Mamie tries to intervene, causing a crisis between Julia and Albert. He fears she is drifting from him; she fears he is only interested in her inheritance. Luckily, the young couple achieves a moment of intimacy in which he admits to feelings of inadequacy and she confesses her anxieties over money. Recognizing their need to begin anew, they decide to move to Houston and start over, distant from Mamie.

In the final act, Mamie makes one last attempt to seduce Albert by poisoning his mind with references to Less Roberts, who lives in Houston. She even offers to make Albert a business partner while she vacations in Louisiana, leaving the house to the children. Suddenly Mr. Borden intervenes and unexpectedly admits to his extramarital affair; at the same time he entreats Julia to find the courage to go away with Albert. As Julia commits to separating from her mother—even at the risk of losing her marriage—Albert decides to join her, which leaves Mamie with only her prosperous oil well. She has her money and her work, so she represses hurt and loss, singing her "endless inward chant" of self-absorption.[4]

Only the Heart is a political play. It includes rumors of the Klan's pursuit of Mr. Borden and his lover. And money motivates all the characters, who have been made especially insecure by the recent chaos and false hopes generated by World War I. As Mr. Borden comments, "During the war, hearing all the hopes of cooperation and change, I thought we would give up our old mistakes—our old ways of doing things. Never turn back, find the way to do different. . . . Once we were spared we couldn't get back to our grabbing quick enough. Well, we deserve what we get—all of us— forgetting once we were spared."[5] Foote's characterization allows us to view a tormented man whose personal demon—passivity—leads him to imagine political history as a record of failed moral courage. Political realities in *Only the Heart* are colored by the consciousness of each character.

The implications for Foote's political vision are profound. Although social realities are often unjust, a deeper terror comes from the confusion and fear with which individuals observe, feel, and interpret those events. Borden, a fumbler, sees the war as the absence of effective action, and Mamie, narcissistic and mildly paranoid, makes foreign relations into the

4. Horton Foote, *Only the Heart* (New York, 1944), 66.
5. Ibid., 32.

story of chronic ingratitude—she instructs Albert that "people don't appreciate your trying to be nice to 'em. They'll turn against you every time when you try to help 'em. . . . Why, look at how those foreign countries we tried to help and loan money are acting."[6] In Foote plays like *Only the Heart,* social attitudes can never be separated from the imaginations that shape them. Even the best political actions can be undermined by the vagaries of well-intentioned persons.

Because he believes so strongly in the capacity of the human mind to create its own reality, to make its heaven and hell, Foote uses political belief as a dramatic projection of his characters' psychology. Without denying the reality of and the need for political action, the writer investigates how an individual's need for intimacy inspires or thwarts responsible, effective social behavior. His plays, teleplays, and films study the complex, self-expressive and also self-justifying ways in which characters advocate a political vision, explicit or implicit, and then make it real by their action or inaction. Without didacticism or dogma, Foote creates a distinctive vision of the relation between the universal need for intimate connection—and the powerful sense of security and well-being it fosters—and humane, just behavior toward others. It is Horton Foote's politics of intimacy.

Mary Hunter (Wolf), the director of *Only the Heart,* understood this quality in Foote's work when she staged the play. In her foreword she explains that Mamie is "externally admirable and attractive, lively—humorous in the lightly sarcastic vein—enterprising—gallant—eager to advise, to help." But, the director continues, the drama actually "lies in the inner activity of the characters, not in the events." Within Mamie Borden lies the tragic irony that her manipulation of others is not mean-spirited; her need to control—like her political belief—is a perversion of a primal drive for "closeness." Mamie can tolerate intimacy only if it does not threaten her rigid sense of self; as Mary Hunter explains, "all her dynamic qualities are turned to manipulation of the people around her into a position of dependency in which her control is absolute. The reason is a tragic one—a deep fear of the give-and-take of love and the closeness of healthy personal relationships. In her own tragic and misguided way she is searching for that love and closeness through the mistaken means of making herself essential as a provider, as a controller of the destinies of those around

6. Ibid., 39.

her." At the end of the play Mamie remains isolated from others, urging Albert to become as independent as she: "Don't let people get at you, hurt you. Learn to live without them. That's the only way to get through life."[7]

Mamie drives her daughter and son-in-law away because she never confronts her failure to be intimate. Allergic to the spontaneity and closeness of dancing, Mamie retreats from what she sees as an essentially unhappy world into the pseudo-security of money: "I reckon we could stand anything if we had a few oil wells." She replaces her own needs with manipulating others and possessing "things": "I'm gonna see that Julia gets all there is to get. Things you can see and touch and feel, things that are there, ready to take care of you no matter what your husband does, or what happens." This need to own and protect leads to her manic pursuit of work: "Everyone's got to learn to take care of themselves. And working is the finest thing in the world, if folks only knew—nothing can get at you— nothing, if you're busy, if you're working." Despite her failure as a mother, Mamie is not an evil person. Her self-possession becomes a personal tragedy because it signifies an inability to love. As India explains to Julia, "You have to love to be loved. Your Mama has forgotten that in her loneliness, her desperation, she has tried to run everything—people, tenants, farmers, me, your Papa, you, now Albert." Mamie's tyrannies begin with, and are expressions of, her fear of intimacy.[8]

Even Foote's best characters are tempted by this fear. In *The Death of the Old Man,* a "camera eye" experiment for television's *Gulf Playhouse* in July of 1953, the audience assumes the point of view of Will Mayfield, a man on his deathbed. According to Rosa (Will's daughter) and others in the play, Will has always followed a selfless, loving path; he has believed "in investin' my money in livin' things. I believe in helpin' the poor an' the unfortunate." As he observes the deception and backbiting among his children over their inheritance, however, Will is tempted to rise up and reclaim material comfort; in a moment of frustration he begs the viewer, "Let me out of this bed . . . let me out. . . . I'll work again. I'll fill the banks with money. I'll buy houses and land and protect us from the dark days because kindness has gone from the world, generosity has vanished."[9] In

7. Mary Hunter, Foreword to *Only the Heart,* 7; Foote, *Only the Heart,* 72.
8. Ibid., 27–28, 29, 31, 67, 72.
9. Foote, *Selected One-Acts,* 135, 141.

Horton Foote's imaginative world, obsessive materialism indicates a failure of kindness and generosity, which have the potential to transform society.

Whereas Will in *The Death of the Old Man* regains his hope and claims a peaceful death, Luther Wright in *The Prisoner's Song* acts out his misplaced feelings. After the death of his daughter, Mary Martha Wright, Luther erects an expensive tombstone to mark her grave. Gripped by sentimentality and the inability to embrace deep loss, Wright pursues Mae Murray, a married woman from a lower class, repeatedly asking her to sing "The Prisoner's Song," the dead child's favorite. Under the spell of his rigid obsession, the wealthy man promises interviews and jobs for Mae's husband, John, in order to keep Mae and her song close. Wright delays and rationalizes throughout the play, and the curtain falls with John still jobless and Mae still singing for Luther Wright. A parable about the roots of politically motivated violence, *The Prisoner's Song* explains the seduction and control of the poor by the rich in terms of failed intimacy.[10]

This reciprocity between personal needs and social action is made explicit in *Drug Store, Sunday Noon,* a commissioned television play from 1956. In the first act Mrs. Lang, immediately after declaring that Otis Taylor has "a wicked tongue and a pig's worth of brains," reminds herself and others that "you'd have an evil tongue, too, if you were Otis Taylor ending up living and raising your girls in a basement house the Chambers built to store vegetables in, always seeing the great big grey house of the Chambers standing before you, up against the sky." She quickly explains, however, that alienation and irresponsibility begin with failed intimacy. As soon as Mrs. Lang asserts, "You got to take care of yourself in this world. Nobody else is gonna take care of you," she reveals the source of her defensiveness. She adds, "Least of all your children. They either steal from you, or if they're any good at all, they get out of town. Nothing to hold them here."[11] Fear and anger, in Foote's vision, pollute both private and public environments.

Because Foote also believes in the power of the human mind when

10. Ibid., 394–413. The recent play *Vernon Early* describes yet another variation on the private-feelings/public-behavior theme. Like Mamie Borden, Vernon has a shallow personal life; he offers almost no closeness to his desperately lonely wife. But unlike Mamie, he compensates by serving Harrison as a caring, respected doctor.

11. Horton Foote, *Drug Store, Sunday Noon,* Act I, 7, 8–9 (MS in Foote Papers).

strengthened by love, dramas like *Only the Heart* imply that a norm exists for effective political action. One must begin with a clear-headed and rigorous acceptance of the fallen, chaotic nature of social reality. This is the lesson implied in Elizabeth's conversation with Horace Jr. in *The Death of Papa*, the last of the nine plays in the *Orphans' Home* series. The subject is Gertrude, a black woman:

> *Horace, Jr.* Is Gertrude poor?
> *Elizabeth.* Yes.
> *Horace, Jr.* Why?
> *Elizabeth.* Because she hasn't any money.
> *Horace, Jr.* Does her mother have money?
> *Elizabeth.* No.
> *Horace, Jr.* Why?
> *Elizabeth.* Because she doesn't get paid much.
> *Horace, Jr.* She works hard?
> *Elizabeth.* Yes.
> *Horace, Jr.* Why doesn't she get paid then?
> *Elizabeth.* Because that's how things are.[12]

Authentic living begins for Foote's characters when they face the reality of "how things are."

Acceptance, however, does not necessarily lead to paralysis. The courage to act responsibly should follow insight. In *Only the Heart*, for example, when Julia fears that she cannot leave her mother's protection and choose her own life, Aunt India reminds her of the power of choice:

> *Julia.* But I'm made of that past. Its ugliness. Its complications
> . . . It's creeping all around me, smothering me . . .
> *India.* For God's sake, Julia, don't let anything frighten you
> into believing you can't choose rightly. The past will do
> that. It's done it to me. It screams out "It's all so compli-
> cated. No use in trying. Let it alone." We had moments
> when we could have done differently, chosen different

---

12. Horton Foote, *"Cousins" and "The Death of Papa": Two Plays from The Orphans' Home Cycle* (New York, 1989) [hereinafter cited as *Two Plays*], 148–49.

ways, and we didn't. That's our past. This is your moment. This is your time to choose.[13]

The need to act—to struggle with one's personal and social history—is crucial, for without it, the endless pursuit of identity and responsibility is impossible.

In Foote's theater of intimacy, one's ability to choose—always political—is valueless if it leads to isolation, a great antagonist. To be fully satisfying, the choices need to bring the characters into communion with their
race or class, their place or religion, and their loved ones. If Foote's people
choose well, they will recognize their ties to and their dependence on family, the land, and tradition. With this sense of connection and place comes
judgment and control, and the courage to be oneself and to face death.
Without it, no genuine contentment, no fully human experience is possible. Foote finds the key to effective political action in healthy attachments,
personal responsibility, and commitment to a fallen, confusing world beyond one's control. In the hard world of Horton Foote's imagination,
nothing less is sufficient.

Foote's most concise expression of this relationship between intimacy
and politics is *The Dancers,* a one-act play produced on the *Philco Television
Playhouse* on March 7, 1954. Set in Foote's fictional town of Harrison,
Texas, in the early summer of 1952, it begins with the arrival of a young
man, Horace, who has come to visit his older sister, Inez Stanley. The political intrigue is stimulated when Inez conspires with Elizabeth Crews, a
wealthy friend, to arrange a date between Horace and Elizabeth's daughter
Emily, generally acknowledged to be the prettiest and most popular girl in
town. Inez is a social climber who wants powerful connections with the
more fashionable and affluent members of Harrison society, and Elizabeth
wants to use Horace to sabotage Emily's romance with Leo, a local boy
unacceptable to the mother. Fortunately, Horace meets Mary Catherine
Davis at a drugstore, and their closeness inspires rebellion against his sister
and the power of privilege. He finds the courage to take Mary Catherine,
not Emily, to the dance.

But there is one more complication. As the young couple get to know
each other, plan their date, and practice the dance steps, they return to the

13. Foote, *Only the Heart,* 66.

issue of confidence, a motif repeated throughout the play. Horace is the first to admit his neediness.

> *Horace.* Well . . . It may sound silly and all to you . . . seeing I'm about to start my first year at college . . . but I'd like to ask you a question . . .
> *Mary Catherine.* What is it, Horace?
> *Horace.* How do you get confidence?
> *Mary Catherine.* Well, you just get it. Someone points it out to you that you lack it and then you get it . . .
> *Horace.* Oh, is that how it's done?
> *Mary Catherine.* That's how I did it.
> *Horace.* You see I lack confidence. And I . . . sure would like to get it. . . .
> *Mary Catherine.* In what way do you lack confidence, Horace? . . .
> *Horace.* Oh, in all kinds of ways. [*A pause.*] I'm not much of a mixer. . . .
> *Mary Catherine.* I think you're mixing just fine tonight.
> *Horace.* I know. That's what's giving me a little encourage-ment. You're the first girl I've ever really been able to talk to. I mean this way.[14]

Confidence is the teenage word for courage in *The Dancers,* a courage in-spired by intimate moments of deep sharing, often of embarrassing emo-tions.

Two scenes later, very near the end of the play, Mary Catherine confides in Horace that she has a weakness, too, a twin of his:

> *Mary Catherine.* I haven't told you the whole truth, Horace. This is my first dance too. . . .
> *Horace.* Is it?
> *Mary Catherine.* Yes. I've been afraid to go. Afraid I wouldn't be popular. The last two dances I was asked to go and I said no.

14. Foote, *Selected One-Acts,* 257.

Horace. Then why did you accept when I asked you?
Mary Catherine. I don't know. I asked myself that afterwards.
I guess because you gave me a kind of confidence.[15]

The Dancers dramatizes how all people sometimes feel inadequate and alone. But this lack of confidence, born of demon fear, can also become a source of transformation.

By sharing their insecurities with caring others who empathize from their own uncertain places, Horace and Mary Catherine find courage. In these intimate moments they discover the capacity to act vitally and to create sane, free lives for themselves. In *The Dancers* Horton Foote dramatizes what Paul Tillich names "acts of courage in which we affirm the power of being, whether we know it or not. If we know it, we accept acceptance consciously. If we do not know it, we nevertheless accept it and participate in it. And in our acceptance of that which we do not know the power of being is manifest to us. Courage has revealing power, the courage to be is the key to being-itself."[16] For both Foote and Tillich, courage transforms impotent knowledge into effective action, and deadening passivity into graceful acceptance. Vitalized by intention and passion, whether thoughtful or participatory, courage sanctifies human experience.

But there is still one other danger in *The Dancers*. Once the couple have found love and courage, they are tempted to cling to each other and turn inward, forming a bond that feels good but forms a deathlike isolation. This is the temptation facing Horace and Mary Catherine in the last moments of the play.

> *Mary Catherine.* You gave me confidence and I gave you confidence. What's the sense of getting confidence, Horace, if you're not going to use it?
>
> > [*A pause. They continue dancing.*]
>
> *Horace.* That's a pretty piece.
> *Mary Catherine.* Yes, it is.
>
> > [*A pause. They dance again.* Horace *stops.*]
>
> *Horace.* I'm ready to go if you are, Mary Catherine.

15. Ibid., 264.
16. Paul Tillich, *The Courage to Be* (New Haven, 1952), 181.

Mary Catherine. I'm ready. [*They start out.*] Scared?
Horace. A little.
Mary Catherine. So am I. But let's go.
Horace. O.K.
[*They continue out the area down the C. of the stage and off
D.R. as the music from the dance is heard . . . and the lights
fade.*][17]

By going to the dance, Horace and Mary Catherine show their readiness
to move beyond their safe, sweet, very private selves; once they share their
fears, they are more able to cross the threshold into the dark unknown beyond the lighted stage. Intimacy offers not just security but also a renewed
spirit of adventure and peace in the public and political world.

In *The One-Armed Man,* which has all the trappings of a political melodrama, the issues are similar. Ned McHenry, disabled in an accident at a
cotton gin, returns to confront his ex-boss, C. W. Rowe. Rowe's previous
exploitation of Ned is clear, as is his present desire to avoid conflict by pay-
ing him five dollars a week. Behind Rowe's sweet Horatio Alger views lies
a cold and distant heart, a man willing to use the powerless in the community, black and white, while lecturing them about their personal and financial habits. But Ned's revenge—he shoots Rowe and at the end of the
play is about to kill Rowe's assistant, Pinkey—is no better. Rowe, for all
his wickedness, is correct in telling Ned that others have learned to deal
with handicaps. Ned handles personal problems no better than Rowe handles social ones. Rather than focus only on social evils, Foote looks at a
more fundamental breakdown of community which implicates both
men.[18]

At the other, healthier extreme is Horace Robedaux in the *Orphans'
Home* cycle. The owner of a clothing business, Horace accepts financial
losses, and even risks economic failure, because he serves black customers.
A paradigm of effective political action, Horace's decision is based on both
personal integrity and social justice. It is especially courageous in the face
of the opportunism that dominated the 1920s. Rather than abandon his
place or reject the cotton-burdened people of Harrison in 1925, Horace

17. Foote, *Selected One-Acts,* 264.
18. Ibid., 418–28.

acts responsibly within his community. In the context of Foote's works, Horace's service to his black clientele is an alternative to Ned McHenry's narcissism and C. W. Rowe's exploitativeness.

In a few rare moments, the writer imagines a world remade by the powerful actions of upstanding people like Horace. For example, in the "Behold a Cry" section from the early play *Out of My House* (1942), Robedaux explains the patient way to face and cure social injustice; he asks Jack to wait until people become "so selfish, so hating, so hideous" that "men everywhere will see clearly how wrong they are. . . . Then men will not be afraid, then they will not hesitate to say . . . this is wrong. This doesn't pay. We can help one another not through fear, but through understanding. Your need is my need, your hunger is my hunger, your loneliness is my loneliness." This visionary voice suggesting a radical return to empathy, comfort, and healing is echoed in Lyndon Johnson's notes on "The Great Society," read by Sam Johnson in Foote's unproduced screenplay *Lyndon:* "there is a new day coming in America, when schoolboys will find new joy that captures and thrills them in discovering and developing their own native capacities, quite as much as in baseball or football, when achievements in nobility, and in creative living, in making friends and in holding them, will crowd crime off the front pages of our newspapers."[19] In a rhetoric not his own, Foote envisions a revolution in the way people treat each other, for only by genuinely "making friends and holding them" can social justice be established and maintained.

This political vision, discovered in subtext rather than text, is also expressed in Foote's films—adaptations as well as original work. In *To Kill a Mockingbird* Foote recreates the tragic story of a small southern town where racism is inflamed by poverty and social ignorance. *Mockingbird* is not content merely to report the violence of Bob Ewell and the unjust conviction of Tom Robinson, however. Its political subject is integrated into Scout's narrative of growing up female in the South. Foote emphasizes that *Mockingbird* is a memory play in which Scout recalls her search for a consciousness that will allow for her tomboy assertiveness and the creativity which produces her story. This search, she remembers, was made especially difficult because her white surrogate mothers were too fastidious and Cal—her source of order and morality—was a black woman.

19. Horton Foote, *Out of My House,* Act IV, 20; and *Lyndon,* Act II, 81.

To Kill a Mockingbird studies and celebrates Scout's return to her past for strength and inspiration. Despite the death of her mother, her brother's restraints on her freedom, and her father's adult remoteness, the narrator survives and flourishes. As she remembers it, the key is found in her ability to control fear—expressed in the children's early terror of Boo Radley—and transform it into the loving assertion "Boo was our neighbor." It is a change made possible by her belief in Atticus, a father who also suggests a loving God, who she remembers was "in Jem's room all night. And he would be there when Jem waked up in the morning."[20] This faith is the best assurance in a dark, inverted world where justice is attained only when Atticus and the sheriff conspire to ignore the rules of the social order. The most potent revolution in *To Kill a Mockingbird* is in Scout's mind, where all revolutions begin.

Tomorrow—adapted from a William Faulkner story—provides a similar political context for the study of intimacy. A detective story shaped by one man's need to know why a lone juror, Fentry, blocks a verdict in a murder case, the internal narrative—almost wholly created by Foote—is a parable-like recounting of Fentry's Christmas love for a pregnant runaway, their marriage, and Fentry's loss of the boy to his wife's family—under the law. Once again, as in *To Kill a Mockingbird,* injustice is supported by social convention and the bond between parent and child inspires the pursuit of justice. Effective, courageous political action is made possible—this time within the law—by the love Fentry gives first Sarah and then Jackson and Longstreet (a.k.a. Buck Thorpe).

These same themes appear in Foote's original screenplays. In *Baby, the Rain Must Fall,* a film version of his play *The Traveling Lady,* class is both brutal and seductive. Henry Thomas has been threatened, beaten, and emotionally abused by Kate Dawson, an influential matriarch in Henry's hometown. In response the boy, a "string band" player of limited talent, pursues a fantasy of Cadillac cars, Hollywood, and Elvis Presley fame—images of social power. But the central drama is not so much physical or external; it is whether Henry's disconnection and early childhood betrayals will keep him from rejoining his wife, Georgette, and their daughter, Margaret Rose. Unfortunately, in this film Henry returns to alcohol, which leads him to attack a jealous man at a dance and then, more gruesomely,

20. Foote, *Three Screenplays,* 80.

Kate Dawson in her grave. Failed intimacy in one's past makes present social responsibilities impossible.

Although written twenty years later, *Tender Mercies* reprises the story of an alcoholic singer facing social and personal crises. His drinking has stripped away Mac Sledge's fame and influence. His songs are rejected by his ex-wife, Dixie, a successful country and western singer, and Dixie's manager—controlled by her responses—also dismisses Mac's new music. Economic hardship pressures Mac toward the violence that destroyed Henry Thomas. Fortunately, Mac's marriage to Rosa Lee and his commitment to her child, Sonny, save him from self-destruction. Unlike Dixie, who surrounds herself with narcissistic fantasies and conspicuous wealth, Mac chooses to share his feelings of abandonment and loss (over the death of Sue Anne, the daughter of Mac and Dixie) with his wife, Rosa Lee. In this case, and in direct contrast to *Baby, the Rain Must Fall,* intimacy holds its own against the history of injustice.

This focus on intimacy differentiates Foote from other recent American dramatists who study personal integrity in conflict with public morality. Class inequities in the plays of Clifford Odets, for example, are also present in Foote's plays, as is the pollution of personal relations by political corruption—a prominent theme in Arthur Miller's work. But Foote differs from both playwrights in his belief that intimacy offers a key to understanding political realities and in his experiments with a transparent realism which rejects the rhetoric of the well-made play. In his defiance of closure Foote is more like David Mamet, with whom he also shares an awareness of alienation as a source of violence. But he differs from Mamet in the use of language. Foote seems to have a deeper trust in people, for he believes the "imagined and remembered particulars" of language offer "possibilities" for courageous exploration of the self and relationships with others.[21] Thus, beneath the spare and harsh surface of the plays, Foote's language is often lyrical whereas Mamet's is rigorously satirical and tends to examine purposeful miscommunication as the prelude to physical and emotional abuse.

This distinction also differentiates Foote's work in film from that of political filmmakers—like Eisenstein or Godard—who seek to provide a pas-

21. Horton Foote, "What It Means to Be a Southern Writer" (lecture for SECA [Southern Educational Communication Authority], n.p., n.d), 23, Foote Papers.

sive, uninformed audience with a new consciousness. Believing that he writes for people neither emotionally deficient nor politically naive, Foote is an artistic populist, closer to John Ford and other traditional document-arists. He has no fundamental need to change his audience; consequently his films most closely resemble those of François Truffaut, Ingmar Berg-man, and Yasujiro Ozu, filmmakers who examine social realities' influence on intimacy. Although he is much more comfortable with melodrama than Foote, Paul Cox uses visual metaphors in *Cactus* to create a film essay on intimacy as a powerful instrument of change. Eric Rohmer creates charac-ters as emotionally rich as Foote's, but Rohmer writes film parables for so-phisticated audiences capable of realizing his greatest ideal—rational choice.

The radical realist in this group, Foote denies his characters the con-scious insight afforded by Cox and Rohmer. Since Foote believes that life is largely inexplicable, capable of both terrible confusion and wonderful mystery, his characters often remain ignorant of their own motives and choices. Uncertain about their needs and identities, his people are only fit-fully clear in their expression. This gap between feeling and self-awareness in his characters allows for the rich subtext typical of most Horton Foote dramas, enabling his audiences to study the shades of meaning between the characters' experience and their ability to explain themselves.

These differences between Foote and other writers and filmmakers who study the politics of intimacy reflect once again the subtle but substantive influence of Christian Science on Foote's work. According to this church, sin, disease, and death are not expressions of the reality of God. Conse-quently, when spiritual love and example—figured in the lives of Mary and Jesus—are made real through prayer and Christian piety, "transformation and healing" can occur in the present, not in "a future-world salvation, or safety."[22] Significantly, giving and receiving these intimate acts of loving care—in imitation of God—can modify the individual consciousness. Fear and the weakness it engenders are replaced by hope and courage— powerful forces for spiritual, emotional, and physical reawakening.

Conservative in its focus on the individual, Christian Science is never-theless committed to the "healing of society at large." Mary Baker Eddy

22. Stephen Gottschalk, "Christian Science," in *The Encyclopedia of Religion,* ed. Mircea Eliade, Vol. III (New York, 1987), 445; Eddy, *Science and Health,* 39.

explains how the reappearance of hope and courage will naturally lead to the social action necessary for the amelioration of human misery and injustice: "One infinite God, good," will not only establish a general "brotherhood of man" but will eliminate "whatever is wrong in social, civil, criminal, political, and religious codes." Scientists like Horton Foote, believing that the miracles of Jesus demonstrate "the power of . . . divine Love to transform and reshape society," look for "the gradual healing of those elements of thought—like selfishness, pride, and intolerance—which lie behind racial and economic injustice and cause war. As a person's affections become more unselfed and universal, he's also led to support enlightened human measures to combat the ills of society." Meaningful political change is thus predicated on the transformative power of genuine intimacy.[23]

In Horton Foote's theater of intimacy, his characters feel content in their attachments to the land, a job, a religion, or a region. But most often they find communion with intimate friends, relations, and loved ones. In any case, Foote's people are asked to make peace with their place in life, their personality, and their social position. This acceptance leads them to public action which does not increase their emotional distance from people and things. They feel connected to others, and from this connection comes support, less need for judgment or control, and the courage to be oneself.

Political issues in Foote's dramas are almost always judged against this benchmark of intimacy. While never condoning the injustice so prevalent in Harrison and other places, Foote does investigate the psychology of oppression, the reasons individuals and groups control and destroy others. His plays and films are not about political action but nevertheless focus on the correlation between social, racial, and sexual injustice and a lack of primary connection. In Foote's work a loss of empathy and acceptance is the first cause of violence, against either oneself, the natural world, or others. Boundless competition and the obsessive need for wealth are not just political problems; they are also symptoms of a failure of emotion and imagination.

By dramatizing these issues in the subtext of his work, Horton Foote creates a distinctive and subtly complex political vision. He records the in-

23. Gottschalk, "Christian Science," 445; Eddy, *Science and Health,* 340; *Christian Science: A Sourcebook of Contemporary Materials* (Boston, 1990), 246, 254; Gottschalk, *Emergence of Christian Science,* 268.

justice and violence in contemporary American life with a brutal clarity that is only partially softened by the historical contexts and the clipped, restrained dialogue of his plays. He is never indifferent to these subjects, which are implied in his studies of intimacy issues. His personal and family stories are charged with and inextricably tied to their political implications. From Foote's perspective, the battleground for social transformation is always the individual consciousness—either empowered by its capacity for love or paralyzed by its isolation and inflexibility.

5

Reality and Myth

Many people in our day, separated from tradition and often cast out by society, are alone with no myths to guide them, no unquestioned rites to welcome them into community, no sacraments to initiate them into the holy—
and so there is rarely anything holy. *The loneliness of mythlessness is the deepest
and least assuagable of all.* Unrelated to the past, unconnected with the future, we hang as if in mid-air.
                                    —Rollo May, *The Cry for Myth*

The American Actors Company was created in New York City during
1937 to support talented young actors in an ensemble atmosphere. From
early in 1938 until the mid-1940s this experimental group produced, in
addition to classical plays like *The Trojan Women,* work by playwrights
"most characteristic of this country, E. P. Conkle, Paul Green, Lynn Riggs
and Thornton Wilder." This emphasis on American voices expressed a
"primary intention" of the AAC (also called the American Actors Theatre),
whose director, Mary Hunter (Wolf), later described the AAC's work as
an "uncovering of our own cultural roots, and since the members of the

company represented almost a regional survey of the United States, the sources were rich and varied." Inspired by the American Actors Company's focus on regional playwrights, Hunter asked actors to create improvisations expressing the idioms, personalities, and stories of their various places.[1]

One of those actors was Horton Foote. An intense young man and a vigorous, ambitious cofounder of the AAC, Foote responded with characteristic enthusiasm. Mary Hunter remembers that "Horton came in one day with a stack of loose sheets, descriptions of some of the people he knew in Wharton. I was absolutely beside myself with joy. It was exactly what I was looking for: authenticity of American roots, of family life and regional experiences."[2] Encouraged by the director and others, especially Agnes de Mille, the actor—just twenty-three—began describing his region, coastal southeast Texas. A natural storyteller, Foote was immediately successful with both the company and New York audiences.

The first of these improvisational exercises in regional theater was Foote's one-act play *Wharton Dance,* written in 1939. Set in a first-floor passageway leading to an upstairs dance hall in Wharton, the drama focuses on a group of young people concerned for Lyda and Bill, a couple long overdue at a local dance. Warmed by beer drinking, the characters pass cigarettes and listen to songs like "Loveless Love" and "Careless Love." They share the adolescent slang of the day, using expressions like "silly slush," "loco" and "cow," "swell," and "a ring dinger." Above all else, the youngsters are united by their need to dance, write "passionate" notes, avoid Mrs. Davis and the Epworth League, and—most important— protect the absent lovers.[3]

The sexual intrigue of *Wharton Dance* is intensified by the arrival, first, of Mary Grace Roberts, whose husband has recently died, and then of Charley Howard, her lover, who declares his intention to marry a local girl, Euroda. Another young man, Ford, a sexually aggressive provocateur, also drifts in, temporarily luring Frankie Belle, a drunk Baptist Sunday-school teacher, away from her husband. After these two crises pass, the conversation becomes more serious, more worried about the gossiping

1. Hunter, Foreword to *Only the Heart,* 5.
2. Mary Hunter, interview with author, September 29, 1990.
3. Horton Foote, *Wharton Dance,* 1, 3, 5, 10, 28, 31, 4 (MS in Foote Papers).

and social injustice in Wharton. All this posing and speculation drives Jane—one of the early arrivals—to the verge of panic, which the others help her control with dancing, an effective tranquilizer. Finally Lyda and Bill arrive, safe and very much in love; Hulia declares the young people have made "the natives stretch their necks," and they all head upstairs. The trials of Wharton's adolescents pass without violence, but with little resolution either.[4]

The following year (1940) the American Actors Company continued its emphasis on regional theater by offering Foote's first three-act, *Texas Town*, described in the manuscript as "A New American Play." Another rich, complex study of the writer's Texas place, the second play is also set in a small town (not identified as Wharton)—this time at a drugstore on a July morning. As Act I opens, the locals are excited over the arrival of the state's governor, who is unpopular with all the characters except Digger. One of the first visitors is Uncle, a man rich in land who may be having an affair with a "Yellar gal" and who is ridiculed for his stingy ways. Another man, Damon, apparently a bank officer, argues with Digger and then punishes him by foreclosing on his mortgage, dislocating not only Digger but also Hannah, a black man who lives on the contested land. The Judge and Pap speculate that the "Southern white man" can't get ahead any more because of lack of backbone, the influx of foreigners and "common folks," "drinking and running around," "cars," and "too much education."[5]

But the play actually focuses on Carrie, a young woman, and her involvement with two men: Maner, who works in the drugstore, and Ray, who desperately wants to escape his mother and small-town life. The subtext of *Texas Town* is Ray's need to leave what he perceives to be a suffocating environment. The local doctor, an alcoholic, supports the young man's desire to "find a life, a real life, my life—not everybody else's idea of life." Bored and jaded people like Fannie Belle and Tim, Lyd and Red and Tom, sneak off together, and the lucky ones, like Mamie (the subject of *Only the Heart* three years later), find oil. But the most substantial antagonist is Mrs. Case, Ray's mother, who wants to use her children to recover family land "owned before the War" and insists "as long as I've got my boys, I don't need anything else."[6]

4. Ibid., 25, 33.
5. Horton Foote, *Texas Town*, 16, 17, 27–28 (MS in Foote Papers).
6. Ibid., 32, 31, 62.

There are more complications in Act II. A Mrs. Nelson enters, which forces the men to use good manners, and flaunts her financial support of the drugstore. The Judge and Pap rescue Digger and Hannah by assuming the mortgage. And then a preacher, Mr. Samuel Carter, shows up praising the virtues of the town. Unfortunately for Ray, the minister has been sent by Mrs. Case to keep Ray down home. When, in Act III, Ray finally leaves on foot for Houston, he is picked up by a drunk who drives off the road while trying to escape curious locals. Meanwhile Doc tells Mrs. Case she has been selfish and Maner admits he is afraid of the outside world. In the final scenes, when the others learn Ray has died from the accident, Carrie, who has left Maner, offers the only hope: "if freedom is right and true . . . then it can be found anywhere."[7] Even when it is not identified as Wharton, Horton Foote's town lacks responsibility, courage, and flexibility.

This interest by Foote and the American Actors Company in dramatizing the "particular and characteristic" qualities of regional life was not unusual in the pre–World War II United States. Plays like *Wharton Dance* and *Texas Town* reflected a national preference for "realism and the school of common life." For many audiences and critics, the presentation of authentic details from American life had become the goal and standard of theater. Using this realist paradigm, Stark Young praised Foote's 1954 play *The Traveling Lady* for employing speech "true, almost unnoticeably true even, to what I heard and saw in that far-off place [south Texas]": "How often in Texas have I heard those idioms, localisms and voluble outbursts and that ranging vocabulary. . . . It all belonged mostly to plain people and people who lived largely in plain towns and circumstances that were all their own and that belonged to themselves and their region." This "accuracy" also extended, Young argued, to the characters, who seem "instead of being written" to have "merely been standing by." Regional art is better, this aesthetic assumes, because it is more real.[8]

But Horton Foote's early realist impulses in *Wharton Dance* and *Texas Town*—as well as other plays he wrote at the American Actors Company— were not only the result of national interest in regionalism. Even before his first plays, Foote had been pursuing—as an actor—an equally powerful influence on his imagination: the Stanislavsky Method. The most instruc-

7. Ibid., 122.
8. Hunter, Foreword to *Only the Heart*, 6; Young, Foreword to *Traveling Lady*, 5, 6.

tive years for him were 1937–1939, when he simultaneously trained at the Tamara Dayakhanova School and acted at the AAC, where Mary Hunter and others followed the tenets of the Moscow Art Theatre.[9] After he shifted from acting to writing, the young playwright remained loyal to the Method, and in 1944 he worked with the Neighborhood Playhouse and its director, Sanford Meisner, a master of the technique. In addition to these obvious collaborators, Stella Adler encouraged his work in the early years, and Lee Strasberg, who had coached the young actor Horton Foote in Hemingway's *The Fifth Column* in 1940, later directed the writer's play *The Traveling Lady* at the Actors Studio in the mid-1950s.

The Stanislavsky tradition fostered Foote's growth from an early literalism to a more psychological realism. Following that tradition, he rejected the formulaic writing, star vehicles, and happy endings of Hollywood. He preferred idiomatic language and the intimate conversation of everyday speech, and he wanted to mirror the lives of his audiences, not just please them. Most of all, method acting taught Foote to create a density of feelings and motive in his characters, giving them a hidden and sometimes dark life. His plays were, like those of the Actors Studio, "set in a real world, with characters who are complex, ambivalent, layered, recognizable, and every bit as neurotic as the people in the audience."[10]

Dance also contributed to Foote's early realism. Two major choreographers of the time—Agnes de Mille and Jerome Robbins—were especially supportive of Foote's writing, and he worked with them through the 1940s and 1950s. But their choreography, tending toward ballet rather than deeply expressive movement, was not quite as attractive to Foote as that of other artists such as Pearl Primus, whose ethnic materials appealed to Foote's preference for genuine people and places, or Valerie Bettis, whom Foote describes as wanting to transform "realistic theater" by using "more boldly the elements of dance, words, and music."[11]

Very helpful to the young writer were Anthony Tudor and, especially, Doris Humphrey and Martha Graham, who modeled the "seriousness of purpose and the storytelling talents" Foote desired. No playwrights of the

9. Hunter interview.
10. Foster Hirsch, *A Method to Their Madness: The History of the Actors Studio* (New York, 1984), 13.
11. Horton Foote, "Learning to Write" (MS in Foote Papers), 81.

time could, he felt, match their achievements in narrative art. Doris Humphrey emphasized naturalness and balance, creating a more physical theater which appealed to Foote's sense of authenticity. He found her style more "lyric" and "sometimes abstract"; her dance usually featured a "a strong narrative line. She told her stories precisely and movingly." Like all members of the American Actors Company, the writer was drawn to Martha Graham's American themes and desire to express an "inner state." According to Foote, Graham portrayed "a dark world of anguish and conflict," personal and psychological. By following these "pioneers of modern dance," the writer was finding a way "to portray the human situation as it really was."[12]

Foote's use of dance is exemplified in two plays written in the mid-1940s. The first manuscript, titled *Daisy Speed,* is listed as a "ballet choreographed and danced by Valerie Beddis [*sic*] numerous times." *Daisy Speed* was actually produced in 1943 as *Daisy Lee,* the story of a woman "twisted by suffering and pain" after the funeral of her husband. Grief, however, does not burden her as much as the "Voices" from the town that describe her unhappy marriage. They say she once was "lovely," "rich and proud," "Beautiful. Very much in love" but in later years has become "filthy, cranky, hardly civil." Throughout the play Daisy tries unsuccessfully to play a song she used to perform for her husband "to show that she loved him." As the dance-play develops, she is visited by the ghosts of her mother—who warns her against marrying "A drunkard. A gambler"—and sister, who at twenty hung herself in despair over an unhappy marriage made in emulation of Daisy. This sister also tempts her to "Curse" the husband around town, in order to "bring you peace and friendship, take away your lonliness [*sic*]."[13]

The short play culminates with the appearance the ghost of Daisy's husband, Charlie. He initially pretends to help her remember their song of reconciliation, for she can recall only a simple phrase. But his "cold insis-

12. Ibid., 80; Doris Humphrey, *The Art of Making Dances* (New York, 1959), 110–15; Foote, "Learning to Write," 79; John Martin, *America Dancing* (New York, 1936), 204; and Agnes de Mille, *Martha: The Life and Work of Martha Graham* (New York, 1991), 207; Foote, "Learning to Write," 79; Dawn Lille Horwitz, "Modern Dance," in *The Dance Catalog,* ed. Nancy Reynolds (New York, 1979), 136.

13. Horton Foote, *Daisy Speed,* 1, 3, 7, 2, 4, 5, 6 (MS in Foote Papers).

tent" mocking is so disturbing that she cannot continue, cannot discover the melody in her love song. Finally Charlie drops his sarcasm and facade of concern, declaring, "I hated our life together. I always hated it. You knew it. You wouldn't let yourself admit it. But you knew it. . . . I hated you and you hated me." Like Georgette Thomas in *The Traveling Lady,* Daisy insists out of loyalty and fantasy that she had saved Charlie from "a drunken grave": "I took care of you. I know you had hard luck. I didn't mind, Charlie. No one knows it better than me and I wouldn't complain. Never. Only don't listen to them and come repeating what they say. Don't." He responds by calling her a "Liar" and begins once again to hum the tune that disorients her. As the play closes, she still cannot remember the song. Even in this early play for dance and music, Foote imagines a dark world where the man is cold and the woman full of delusions.[14]

In the 1944 dance-play *The Lonely,* choreographed by Martha Graham, Foote employs an even darker realism. This story focuses on Sam Mann, who moments before his death admits that he has "always a great fear of loneliness" and wants to know before he dies "why such a thing have [*sic*] to be." Sam's sadness is shared by the other characters who describe loneliness as "a disease eating at our hearts." The result is a general malaise in which, as an early stage direction clarifies, "All the figures move with open and violent despair." Sam's wife and his brother Tom are infected by this despair, as are *The Lonely*'s bridge players, who change seats after each hand, and the bartender, who repeatedly tosses a ball with women in the bar. Empty of genuine religious feeling, the characters mechanically recite the Lord's Prayer—which in no way impedes their drinking bouts and seductions.[15]

The result is a dance of death. The waltz in this play has none of the powerful grace it has in, for example, *Courtship.* In *The Lonely* no one is committed or content; each dancer is "searching for a new partner." The recurring theme of class violence—which is more refined and subtle in later Foote plays—is obvious and intrusive here; the bridge players run off the prostitute, declaring, "Here you will find only the best people." Worst of all, the preacher who shows up late in the dance-play is ineffectual, minis-

14. Ibid., 8, 9.
15. Horton Foote, *The Lonely,* 2, 6, 1 (MS in Foote Papers).

tering in compliance to a wrathful God: "Let us not mock God by asking reasons. Accept. Let us accept. Joyfully, willingly. . . . Ask not. Question not." His God asks only obedience, not intimacy and joy.[16]

The American Actors Company offered Foote much more than a place to write his first dramas. It initiated him into the new realism—in regionalism, method acting, and modern dance—that became the basis for his later stories "true to their place and time."[17] But, as Foote soon learned, and as he has been implicitly arguing ever since, there are limits to a writer's impulses toward realism. Dialogue must be both idiomatic and poetic, historical characters must be modified for legal and formal reasons, and stories eventually find their own structures and endings, which may or may not reflect the intention, or will, of the writer. In order to avoid local color— flat regionalism—the writer must modify his or her realistic impulses, to grow as an artist; despite early critical approval, Foote judged his earliest work mere reporting that lacked the resonance of a personal vision.[18]

Throughout the 1940s—and to some degree ever since—Foote has been wrestling with a paradox central to the craft of any realist. Describing real events and characters can be truthful and even moving, but imaginative art requires that these facts be placed in more than regional contexts. Naturalism presumes that human behavior and emotional responses are largely the result of environmental influences. The metaphor of animal behavior informs the language and rhetoric of its realism. Similarly, historical fiction appears to retell only actual events while always assuming a rational and causal relationship between those events. Even postmodern realist writing often asserts the integrity of the individual consciousness while embracing disorder and relativity. As minimalist as their art may sometimes be, realists must struggle with the specter of literalism; they must

16. Ibid., 15, 8, 19, 13, 18.

17. Horton Foote, Introduction to *"Roots in a Parched Ground," "Convicts," "Lily Dale," "The Widow Claire": The First Four Plays of "The Orphans' Home" Cycle* (New York, 1988) [hereinafter cited as *Four Plays*], xv.

18. Mary Hunter also understood the limits of the regionalism she fostered in writers like Horton Foote. In his SECA lecture "What It Means to Be a Southern Writer," Foote notes that she "made me understand . . . that relying on a sense of place, no matter how accurately, was not enough, if as a writer you didn't only want to be content with quaintness and parochialism" (p. 14). Similarly, dance, while it encourages authentic American storytelling, also at times emphasizes abstract, less "regional or . . . folk" elements, as Foote noted in his Fairleigh Dickinson College lecture, pp. 11–12.

venture beyond the thing itself—into the world of vision and meaning—without desecrating the sanctity of the living world.

Flannery O'Connor explained this realist paradox—in terms of regional literature—when receiving the Georgia Writers' Association Scroll. The truth of a place, O'Connor explains, "is not made from the mean average or the typical, but from the hidden and often the most extreme. It is not made from what passes, but from those qualities that endure, regardless of what passes, because they are related to truth. It lies very deep. In its entirety, it is known only to God, but of those who look for it, none gets so close as the artist."[19] Art, even the most particular and real, pursues universal truths, which by their nature are "known only to God." Regional writers do not escape the realist paradox; according to O'Connor, they too must transcend their material to join the mystery of art.

This requirement that regional writing be more than literal explains Foote's recurrent interest in and profound respect for Katherine Anne Porter, particularly her story "Noon Wine." In her essay on the sources of that story, which Foote often quotes, she describes the necessary transformation of truthful, authentic matters in the pursuit of art. She reminds readers that in the "endless remembering which surely must be the main occupation of the writer, events are changed, reshaped, interpreted again and again in different ways, and this is right and natural because it is the intention of the writer to write fiction, after all—real fiction, not a *roman à clef*, or a thinly disguised personal confession which better belongs to the psychoanalyst's séance."[20] Katherine Anne Porter and Horton Foote, like the best regional writers, recognize that it is "right and natural" for art to change and reshape the real world. They both write "real fiction."

19. Flannery O'Connor, *Mystery and Manners* (New York, 1980), 58.

20. Katherine Anne Porter, *The Collected Essays and Occasional Writings of Katherine Anne Porter* (Boston, 1970), 468. In "Learning to Write," 90, Foote recalls that reading Porter's collection *Pale Horse, Pale Rider* "had a profound and lasting effect on me. Here it seemed to me was a supreme prose stylist, yet with no trace of artifice. No local colorist and not sentimental about the past, and yet using the past and the region of her birth to create her imagined world." While Porter and Foote both believe in the ordering principle of art, Porter advocates a classical "feeling of reconciliation—what the Greeks would call catharsis, the purification of your mind and imagination—through an ending that is endurable because it is right and true"; Barbara Thompson, *Writers at Work* (New York, 1963), 157. There is no "right and true" resolution in Foote's plays; the quality of life, its closeness to natural rhythms, is his artistic norm.

As Porter and Foote cross the line from the real to the fictional, they study the uses of myth in contemporary life and art. For Foote, secular myth is often riddled with illusion, drawing people away from the deeper, often darker, realities of human experience. Consequently, much of his work verges on satire, revising traditional social mythology in favor of his own brand of humanism. In stories like *The Chase* and *The Traveling Lady* he critiques the radical individualism often expressed by west Texas writers. Foote relies instead on authentic stories from east Texans who value family and community over personal expression. For Foote's characters, identity is discovered in groups, not isolation; consequently he demythologizes the cowboy's reverence for isolation.

Foote becomes even more closely aligned to Porter when his plays move beyond their critique of popular myth and offer a Christian subtext as a norm for judging characters and their behavior. The integration of sacred stories, whether explicit or implied, is a declaration of faith wherein religious myths have the power to—as Joseph Campbell believes—"lead the young from their estate in nature, and . . . bear the aging back to nature and on through the last dark door. And while doing all this, they . . . render an image of the world of nature . . . that should seem to support the claims and aims of the local social group; so that through every feature of the experienced world the sense of an ideal harmony resting on a dark dimension of wonder should be communicated."[21] Those who participate in the mythos are initiated into society without losing a sense of wonder; they become part of the eternal cycle of separation from and return to nature. Those who do not, it is implied, live essentially placeless lives.

Christian mythology in the realistic fiction of Porter and Foote, like that of fellow southerners Flannery O'Connor and William Faulkner, reflects southern writers' creative obsession with what Lewis Simpson calls the "historicizing of time," the disjunction between communal myth and personal experience. This loss of context haunts these modern storytellers who, according to Flannery O'Connor, need sacred guides, "something to measure" themselves against: "For the purposes of fiction, these guides have to exist in a concrete form, known and held sacred by the whole community. They have to exist in the form of stories which affect our image

21. Joseph Campbell, "Mythological Themes in Creative Literature and Art," in *Myths, Dreams, and Religion,* ed. Joseph Campbell (New York, 1970), 144.

and our judgment of ourselves. Abstractions, formulas, laws will not serve here. We have to have stories in our background. It takes a story to make a story. It takes a story of mythic dimensions, one which belongs to everybody, one in which everybody is able to recognize the hand of God and its descent."[22] Because these writers are preoccupied with the loss of legendary stories, ones "held sacred by the whole community," they are all mythic realists, yearning to find universal contexts for their specific and regional tales. It is in this tradition that Horton Foote writes and finds his distinctive literary voice.

As O'Connor implies, mythic realism asserts that stories, when held sacred by their culture, have the power to give order and meaning to human experience. In times of faith, literature bridges the profane and the sacred, sanctifying life and offering models of morality and courage. When—as in the modern age—faith recedes and the material world feels disconnected from the purpose and contentment of a spiritual one, the reiteration of myth becomes a source of imaginative healing. Ideally, with the "re-presentation of the myths the entire community is renewed; it rediscovers its 'sources,' relives its 'origins.' " Writers of this tradition of realism, whether believers or not, value storytelling as a primary existential need. They believe that shared stories, when they gain mythopoeic power, can make human history, in Mircea Eliade's words, "significant, precious, and exemplary."[23]

When practiced in Judeo-Christian contexts, as southern writing often is, mythic realism is distinguished by its preoccupation with "the drama of Paradise."[24] William Faulkner, for example, continually returns to the Fall—in the Bible, the South, and Western civilization—as the primary background, or the general antagonist, in his fiction. It is the single shared

22. Lewis Simpson, *The Fable of the Southern Writer* (Baton Rouge, 1994), 99; O'Connor, *Mystery and Manners,* 202. Mircea Eliade, in *The Myth of the Eternal Return,* trans. Willard R. Trask (New York, 1965), 35, similarly describes "an implicit abolition of profane time, of duration, of 'history' " by myth. Cf. Roland Barthes, who asserts that myth "transforms history into Nature" by abolishing "the complexity of human acts" and establishing "a blissful clarity"; "Myth Today," in *A Barthes Reader,* ed. Susan Sontag (New York, 1982), 116, 132. While Barthes attacks myth for its reductive tendencies, Foote, like Eliade, is concerned with the privatization of experience; narcissism in life and art is his antagonist.

23. Mircea Eliade, *Myth and Reality,* trans. Willard R. Trask (New York, 1963), 6, 20, 30, 35, 19.

24. Ibid., 93.

burden of the Yoknapatawphans of any creed, race, or class. Katherine Anne Porter similarly focuses on the loss of Eden, but she is concerned less with the Fall itself than with the psychological implications which follow. Her writing is preoccupied with man's inevitable betrayal of himself and others—the Judas moment. Porter records man's eternal failure to follow God's commandment to love. In Flannery O'Connor's stories, on the other hand, humanity's fallen nature is so pervasive that it cannot provide the source of dramatic conflict as it does in Porter. O'Connor focuses on the theophanic event: the time when God reveals man's failure and brokenness. In her drama the only hope rests in the protagonist's discovery of his or her sinful state and the necessity of God's grace and mercy. For each of these southern mythic realists the fall from Eden is the central mythic reality, the story before all others.

Although Horton Foote is interested in the loss of innocence, his use of the Fall has a uniquely personal inflection. Unlike Faulkner, Porter, and O'Connor, Foote is not obsessed with the impotence, failure, and ignorance resulting from the loss of Eden; rather, he asserts the power of the human mind to achieve love, identity, and courage. Foote's dramas are decidedly interior; all significant action lies in the emotions of his characters. In this essentially mental theater, the metaphorical exit from Paradise is both natural and necessary for the development of authenticity. Unlike his fellow southern mythic realists, he focuses on ways to return to Edens never imagined by the innocent mind. More like William Blake, Foote imagines other, psychological Edens, just outside the disoriented present; home for him is an ever-changing and never fully realized state of mind, not a place or time in history.

Foote's distinctive theme—his version of the southern fall from grace—is the rite of going away and coming home, the eternal need for both roots and wings. At the onset of his stories, characters find themselves either in Eden, with an emotionally satisfying primary connection, or outside, "parched" by loveless disconnection. When this attachment is inadequate, as it is for Horace Robedaux in *Roots in a Parched Ground,* characters must go away to find the intimacy that has been denied them. Even if the original home has been sustaining and full of love, as it has for Mary Catherine in *The Dancers,* the characters must leave; otherwise they become like Laura Lee in *Night Seasons,* stifled and unindividuated. Without the freedom to go away from home, Foote's characters never achieve the identity essential to their health and peace.

This archetypal need to leave home is the subject of *The Old Beginning,* a one-act teleplay produced by the *Goodyear Theatre* on November 23, 1952. It focuses on a contemporary (1950) story of Tommy Mavis, a young man from the fictional Harrison who must confront a very powerful and influential father, H.T. As the play opens, Tommy has just made the second of two autonomous decisions: he has agreed to rent a property without his father's assistance, soon after becoming engaged to Julia Thornton. His father arrives and insists on checking Tommy's punctuality, asking him to hurry and to be more businesslike. A crisis is precipitated when both Tommy and his father rent an old building in town. The ensuing argument escalates when H.T. calls his son a "numbskull" and then "a little two-bit kid that hasn't sense enough to come in out of the rain." Tommy reacts angrily, telling his father he is "domineering and egotistical and cold-blooded and ruthless," and slams the door as he leaves the office.[25]

The simple, external plot is resolved comically when H.T.'s prospect for the lucrative rental is revealed as a fraud, a mental case who pretends to represent a substantial firm. Tommy decides nevertheless to leave home to "feel free to do what I want." Significantly, his decision is based not on anger but on a clear commitment to his own life, his own risks. Momentarily the boy agrees to work at his father's business while his parents go on a vacation. But when H.T. resumes his manipulations, calling Tommy's decision to move out of the family home "the most ridiculous thing I ever heard of," Tommy exits the business, too, for his "own independence and self-respect." At the conclusion, Tommy and Julia are satisfied with the boy's break from his father and hope that the parents will accept and understand. As Foote's title suggests, this leaving is an "old beginning," one revisited each time innocence is lost in the pursuit of identity and responsibility.[26]

The leave-taking represented in *The Old Beginning* is eventually followed by a need to compromise one's autonomy for an equally archetypal reconnection. Going away in order to discover one's identity leads—in the

25. Horton Foote, *The Old Beginning,* in *Selected One-Acts,* 28, 31–32.
26. Ibid., 42, 43, 21.

best, healthiest scenario—to various roads to man's many homes. Intimacy is most obviously and pervasively rediscovered in loving attachments—now freely chosen—to a family, as in *The Orphans' Home*. Community and religious tradition can serve as well, as they do for Rosa Lee in *Tender Mercies*. Even work, which revitalizes Will Kidder at the end of *The Young Man from Atlanta*, can bring direction and order. Occasionally the land is more a source of faith than people are, as Carrie Watts learns in *The Trip to Bountiful*. In each case, meeting the renewed need for affiliation fulfills a deep longing for peace; without a return to these emotional homes the specter of loneliness reappears in Foote's imaginative worlds.

Foote's trilogy of one-act plays, *The Roads to Home*, demonstrates the necessity of a return from cold independence. The plays center on Annie Gayle, a Harrison girl who has married, had two children, and moved to Houston. In the first play—*A Nightingale*—she obsessively rides streetcars, often to visit a Harrison acquaintance, Mabel Votaugh, and Mabel's friend Vonnie Hayhurst. Troubled by a past marked by her family's unhappy move from the North to Harrison and her father's murder by his best friend, Annie slides into a distractedness in which she neglects her children and husband and is eventually (in the third play, *Spring Dance*) institutionalized in an Austin, Texas, hospital. Along the way—in play two, *The Dearest of Friends*—Vonnie's husband has an affair with a Harrison girl and Annie's husband divorces her and remarries. Most simply, the plays are about people away from home and lost.

This displacement is essentially emotional, rather than geographic. The confusion which dogs the characters results in part from innocent fantasies about the past; in the first play, Annie mechanically sings "My Old Kentucky Home" and is mindlessly nostalgic for "dear old Harrison," when in actuality, back in Harrison the Baptist preacher has run off with another man, murder is committed in the streets, prejudice is institutionalized, and seduction is as real as fidelity. This loss of social and moral grounding is also a religious matter in *The Roads to Home*. In the first play Annie refuses Vonnie's request that she pray: "I don't need prayer. Thank you. I need to be mature and self-reliant, a doctor told me. I need tenderness and mercy." Religion has become perfunctory and coercive; it tends to infantilize rather than encourage maturity. Sadly and ironically, tender and merciful emotions, traditionally the most profound expression of the Christian mythology, are reduced to ineffective medical advice. Annie and the others experience a paralyzing dissociation between human needs and religious experience.[27]

Just as individual lives gain balance and health by incorporating the process of going away and coming home, all life in Foote's dramas seeks the natural rhythm of moving from union to alienation/identity to reunion. The state of innocence noted by Mr. Vaughn at the end of *1918* is eventually replaced by the failures, diseases, and tragedies of human experience. But Foote is never sentimental when writing about this loss, for it is essential to the realism, self-understanding, and courage he values throughout his work. Regardless of whether identity is achieved, his characters find peace in a not wholly unfriendly death. Even if he or she does not understand it, each person returns to a loving God who, according to Foote, experiences time as a divine respiration that embraces every loss and restoration.

But his reliance on the theme of eternal return is not the only way to distinguish Foote from other southern mythic realists. More subtle, and yet more determinative in single plays and films, is Foote's use of Christian myth as a benchmark for the emotions, decisions, and actions of his characters. When characters lack common purpose, the story-ideal reveals their sadly comic isolation from love and community. But when they are moved by loving connections, the stories exemplify the power of intimacy, courage, and peace in the modern world. In every case Foote's dramas reverberate with human possibilities untapped and harmony straining to become real. Although the characters may not choose to listen, the myths continuously offer Horton Foote's most powerful gift—healing.

Two examples—from plays which have become screenplays—indicate how Foote builds subtext from resonant mythology. He uses myth comically in a scene added to the film version of *The Trip to Bountiful*. A bus stops deep in the night, and its passengers congregate aimlessly near the door of an old gas station:

Mrs. Watts. Do you have far to go?
Black Woman. Right far . . . Corpus.
Bus Operator. You know what Corpus Christi means in Spanish?

27. Horton Foote, *The Roads to Home,* in *Selected One-Acts,* 298, 299, 312.

Mrs. Watts. No, I don't.

Bus Operator. Body of Christ.

Mrs. Watts. That so? I never heard that. [*To* Black Woman:] Did you?

Black Woman. No, I sure hasn't. The Body of Christ. Is that right?

[*A* Mexican Man *waits at the other side of the bus stop.* Bus Attendant *calls over to him.*]

Bus Attendant. Is that right?

[*The* Mexican Man *says something in Spanish.*]

Black Woman. I see the bus coming. I sure am glad to see it.[28]

The incongruity and miscommunication among the travelers are both humorous and resonant. The characters are ignorant of more than Spanish and the place names around them; oblivious to stories and religious personages that might offer them common experience, language, and purpose (within Christian mythology), they create a new Babel. Without naming a specific religious ideology, Foote dramatizes the distance between the Christian call to community—represented by the Body of Christ—and the lack of direction in the characters' lives.

On the other hand, a life resembling the Christian stories is, even without a character's understanding, lyrical. In *Tomorrow* Sarah Eubanks, pregnant and orphaned from her husband and family, finds herself at the cabin of Jackson Fentry on Christmas Day. He comforts her, and despite the cold and poverty they become close. Their conversation is seemingly pointless until, just before the baby is born, a rainstorm inspires Sarah: "It's a good thing we don't live on the Delta. We'd just have to get up on top of this house and float away in case it flooded. Well, I don't think I'd care to travel by water. I think I always want to be where I can feel the ground under my feet. Jesus walked on water, they say. Do you believe that? I knew a preacher once; he swore it was true and he said he was gonna do it, too. A whole crowd of folks went down to watch him, but he sank to the bottom."[29]

28. Foote, *Three Screenplays*, 182–83.

29. Horton Foote, *Tomorrow*, in *Tomorrow and Tomorrow and Tomorrow*, ed. David G. Yellin and Marie Connors (Jackson, Miss., 1985), 128–29.

As in the *Bountiful* passage, a humorous incongruity exists between the nature of the physical world and the preacher's arrogance. Sarah's anecdote is especially telling because it amplifies her own insecurities; she wants solid ground, not adventure in a fluid place. Her subconscious introduction of the Flood and Jesus' walk on the water also raises the question of miracles in the modern, material age. A product of the Protestant South, Sarah may have mindlessly reiterated a story she has heard, but the myths speak louder, with more resonance than she. The simple woman has become Mary-like, and Fentry Joseph-like; they are reenacting the transformative power of intimacy told in the biblical story, suggesting that miracles are possible even in this internal, psychological age as long as people love responsibly, with commitment and fidelity.

As these two examples reveal, Foote's writing does not quite create the revealed God of O'Connor or the symbolic resonance of Porter. Foote believes it is presumptuous, even arrogant, for literature to assume an explicitly religious goal. He realizes that didacticism never serves art well. His realism also avoids heavy and detailed literary reference, even when biblical. He uses artistic references sparingly, never wanting the play or film to draw attention to its own artistry. Nevertheless, belief serves Foote's dramatic imagination in an idiosyncratic and personal way. Characters who embrace the writer's most personal myth—the divine cycle of going away and coming home—discover his most sacred emotion: peace. For those who listen intuitively to the stories of the Christian mythology, his dramas offer glimpses of the sacred. And every genuine religious experience—like loving attachments to family, community, work, and the land—provides a source of courage, the primary virtue in his dramas.

Foote's use of story is thus ironically closer to that of William Faulkner, the most secular of the southern mythic realists admired by Foote. In Faulkner, storytelling becomes a means by which one can recover a lost sense of community. The artist momentarily calls individuals back to the shared story, even in a horribly fallen world, allowing literature to become a kind of secular religion. Like Faulkner, Foote believes that shared stories can build community, tradition, and order. The telling qualification, however, is Foote's insistence that mythic stories come from God, not man. A believer, but not an evangelical one, Foote creates characters who are haunted by myth. Whether they know it or not, believe it or not, myths are their hope and salvation.

This mythic realism reveals a creative tension between Foote's public responsibility to report and his private need to believe. A very religious man, he nevertheless consciously and rigorously tries to avoid writing "from that point of view."[30] Most of his characters have no specific religion, or if they do, the stories typically do not deal with personal religious issues, except perhaps peripherally or comically. Even as he suppresses his convictions, not wanting to proselytize or become dogmatic, the power of love remains an unspoken presence, a silent reminder of what is absent and what is needed. The resonance, indirection, and surprising ambiguity in Foote's work result from his artistic compromise between his naturalistic surfaces and his religious subtexts.

Foote's resolution—his vision—is discovered in his use of *myth as healing*. Instead of dogma he offers many seemingly unrelated stories whose diversity camouflages his creative obsession with the cyclical pattern of going away and coming home, experienced both individually and archetypally. Largely unaware of this pattern of freedom and connection, his characters are nevertheless surrounded by language, imagery, and stories informed by Christian mythology. These myths become living presences waiting to be heard and believed; they remain as potential sources of power and order whatever the characters say or do. Myth is eternal, according to Horton Foote, but it always must be willed, made real, by the love of human beings for each other and God.[31]

30. Wood and Barr, " 'Certain Kind of Writer,' " 231.

31. See Eliade, *Myth of the Eternal Return,* 77, who contends that in modern times, "the structure of the myth and the rite remains unaltered . . . even if the experiences aroused by their actualization are no longer anything but profane. . . . All that is needed is a modern man with a sensibility less closed to the miracle of life."

—⬤ 6 ⬤—

The Orphans' Home

This chapter is the first of three to examine how Horton Foote's aesthetic is realized in specific stories. *The Orphans' Home* is a cycle of nine plays written in the mid-1970s and staged throughout the United States beginning at the end of that decade. Initially supported by Peggy Feury on the West Coast and Herbert Berghof (and the HB Theater) in New York, early productions were staged at the Ensemble Studio Theater in Manhattan, the Actors Theater in Louisville, and eventually in regional theaters across the United States. By 1986 Reynolds Price proclaimed the cycle "near the center of our largest American dramatic achievements."[1]

In his introduction to the Grove Press edition of four plays from *The Orphans' Home,* Foote has explained how he wrote the nine stories. Although the first play, *Roots in a Parched Ground,* had appeared fifteen years earlier as a teleplay for the *Du Pont Show of the Month,* the cycle was not inspired by that initial piece but by the death of the writer's parents in con-

---

1. Reynolds Price, "Introduction: New Treasure" to *"Courtship," "Valentine's Day," "1918": Three Plays from "The Orphans' Home" Cycle* (New York, 1987) [hereinafter cited as *Three Plays*], xiii.

secutive years. Foote is exact about the genesis of the cycle: "The actual writing of these plays began after my mother's death in 1974. My father had died the year before in the very room and on the bed my brothers had been born in." Feeling a double loss, the cycles of birth and death, and the ironies of life, Foote attended to the business of transition. In Wharton he spent time alone "sorting letters and personal papers, making decisions about what to do with the accumulations of fifty-nine years of life in that house." Then he returned to his New Hampshire home.[2]

There, surrounded by family and the peaceful woods, he began the story of his father. But he did not return immediately to *Parched Ground*. Instead, he "began making notes" on the whole cycle. Within two years he had completed drafts of eight plays, including a reworking of *Parched Ground*; only *The Widow Claire* was yet to be written. While composing these first drafts, Foote listened continually to the music of Charles Ives. As he remembers, in the winter he wrote beside fires and in the spring and summer he observed the woods and "a large stone wall" outside his window. He does not recall the order of the plays but believes *1918* came first and *The Widow Claire* last.[3]

One other explanation from the writer is especially useful: The initial notes were prompted by his "thinking over my parents' lives and the world of the town that had surrounded them from birth to death." These plays are, before all else, an imaginative record of a place and time in American experience:

> The time of the plays is a harsh time. They begin in 1902, a time of far-reaching social and economic change in Texas. The aftermath of Reconstruction and its passions had brought about a white man's union to prevent blacks from voting in local and state elections. But in spite of political and social acts to hold onto the past, a way of life was over, and the practical, the pragmatic were scrambling to form a new economic order. Black men and women were alive who knew the agony of slavery, and white men and women were alive who had owned them. . . . And so with the 1918 influenza epidemic, which causes such havoc in the play *1918*.[4]

2. Foote, Introduction to *Four Plays*, xi.
3. Ibid., xi–xii.
4. Ibid., xi–xiii.

In these plays, as in all of Foote's work, the sense of historical moment shapes the action. Yet as true as he is to history and as careful as he is with the details and facts, he does not write simply about these things. In *The Orphans' Home* the Vaughns and Robedauxs face diseases and dislocation, confusion, estrangements, and betrayals specific to turn-of-the-century coastal southeast Texas. But Foote's abiding concern here is with the courage to face change, a topic unique to no place or time. In the writer's words, these plays "are about change, unexpected, unasked for, unwanted, but to be faced and dealt with or else we sink into despair or a hopeless longing for a life that is gone." [5]

The process of change in *The Orphans' Home* actually begins before the first play, *Roots in a Parched Ground,* when the children—Horace and Lily Dale—must face the separation of their parents. Confused by this disorder, the children soon learn that the Thorntons, dancing people, and the Robedauxs, bookish people, do not get along much better than the children's parents, Paul Horace and Corella. The death of their father adds more chaos to the children's lives. But Horace's wild flight into a storm is not precipitated by these perceived betrayals; his mother's remarriage and move to Houston, leaving him behind, is his greatest terror. This abandonment, which Horace experiences as a violent rejection, leaves him rootless and alone.

It is not just the parents who fail Horace. Here, as in *The Traveling Lady,* Foote also implicates the town in these unmet responsibilities. Aunt Gladys reassures the young man that he has not only a mother but "a grandmother, a grandfather, aunts, and an uncle to take care of you." George Tyler declares, "We all will want to look out for him." Terrence Robedaux adds, "I'll help him as long as I'm here." And John Howard echoes, "We'll all help you, son." [6] But age, poverty, self-interest, and Horace's compulsive withdrawal cast these promises on parched ground. This Victorian world may worship duty and order, but it is east of Eden. Horace is left to his own resources; he has lost his innocence.

Despite his many painful experiences, the past is what sustains Horace in these times of brokenness. Even before his father dies, the son had been curious about John Howard, Paul Horace's partner, whose two children

5. Ibid., xii.
6. Foote, *Four Plays,* 55, 59.

had died in a fire ten years earlier, leaving their mother a recluse. But Horace's interest in such unhappiness is neither morbid nor depressive. Unlike some of the Robedauxs and Mrs. Howard, he is not condemned to repeat the failures of history. Wishing to know his heritage even when it is unpleasant, he wants to place a tombstone on his father's grave, which his grandmother and his father's friends were unable to do. Like the strongest of Foote's characters, Horace respects the past, but he wants to use it as a source of strength and flexibility in the present. At twelve his struggle with despair, introversion, and self-doubt has begun, as has his search for a new father and home.

By the end of the first play of *The Orphans' Home,* the central issue is no longer blood ties, death, or even abandonment. Although he wishes it were otherwise, Horace's life has become his own. It is unfortunate that his innocence has been lost prematurely, but his predicament is shared by all the characters. George Tyler, who will later lose his mind and commit suicide, is most clear in *Parched Ground* when he explains to Horace, "There's music over there at the Thorntons again. There's been some changes, haven't there? Your daddy's dead, the Robedauxs moved, your mama married again—a lot of changes. Well, we have to get used to change, son. All of us."[7] Despite his many losses, Horace Robedaux will find peace only in the courage to face change.

Horace's fall from innocence continues in *Convicts.* Here, he learns about the lack of kinship and fellow-feeling in his town. Attached to an irrepressible uncle and still trying to save money for his father's gravestone, he goes to work at an old plantation that is in actuality a prison for convicts, apparently all black. At the Gautier Plantation he is introduced to more violence—black against black, between brothers, and within families other than his own. And he discovers, by observing both blacks and whites, that much of this violence is racial. Sherman Edwards shows him the deep hatred blacks feel for the horrors of slavery and the caste system. At the other extreme Soll Gautier, though also a comic and tragic figure, reveals himself as a bitter and violent white racist.

In his relationship with Soll, Horace is forced to deal with psychological, not just social, innocence. Deeply hurt by the loss of his own father and the lack of support from the Thorntons and Robedauxs, the young

7. Ibid., 87.

boy is driven, beneath his calm surface, by an obsessive need for a father. Recognizing Horace's desire to please older, stronger men, Leroy Kendricks, a convict chained to a tree, tries to exploit the boy's weakness by asking him for a knife and directions for an escape. But Soll, the plantation's overseer, is the real focus of Horace's ambivalence. He repeatedly promises to buy "the biggest goddamned tombstone in Texas" for Paul Horace's grave, with "angels on it and two Confederate veterans."[8] At heart a broken man who had no mothering and has lost his friends to death, Soll reneges on these offers, as he does on all others.

Yet it is through Soll that Horace gets the chance to revisit his problems with his father. Though Soll is in some ways an unregenerate human being, Horace by his own admission cannot leave the overseer. This attachment results, in part, from the boy's identification with the old man's hidden vulnerability implied in the facts that Soll's mother died in childbirth and that Soll has nightmares in which blacks repay his violence against them. His closeness to Soll also allows Horace to review his personal history. He learns that class violence and racism haunt the past adored by his relatives, and that despite what whites believe, blacks like Martha Johnson see the evil in men like Soll and are willing to face up to them. Finally, Horace, who was not present at his own father's death, watches Soll die.

Once he discovers that failed intimacy is the basis of his surrogate father's racism, Horace is better able to respect difference and become trustworthy. Despite all the betrayals by this second father, he empathizes with the man's pain and fear. At least Soll respected life enough to, as Ben says, mind dying in "the worst way." And so Horace keeps his promise to "sit by his side with a gun after he died, until he was buried." Inspired by this example, Jackson decides to sing "Golden Slippers," despite the racial stereotyping the words recall. It is the least these men, black and white, can do for a man passing, any man passing, even Soll Gautier.[9]

Unfortunately, Horace's bitterness does not die with Soll. Although his desire to sanctify—by marking their graves—the lives of his father, Soll, and a dead convict signifies his need to forgive his various fathers, his mother is a different case. Her rejection of Horace, her submission to Pete

8. Ibid., 134.
9. Ibid., 161.

Davenport's will, and her implicit preference for Horace's sister remain with Horace even after he has helped bury Soll Gautier. When he leaves the plantation and returns to his biological family, his anger returns with a vengeance. Its poison attacks his body as well as his mind.

That disease is the subject of the next play, *Lily Dale*, in which Horace's train ride from Glen Flora, where he has a new job at the Galbraith store, to Houston and back again is a descent into a kind of personal hell. It is, for him, the end of a fantasy of family. His sister is only half aware of this loss; denial is one of her favorite emotions. Their mother is paralyzed; she feeds Horace and waits for change, but she cannot act. Pete Davenport and his alter ego, Will Kidder, are of no help either, for they despise confusion, dependency, and the past. Instead of the blood ties he longs for, Horace finds only disease, dreams, and an ambiguous call for religion.

Pete clearly does not want Horace in Houston. And when Lily Dale points out, in her provocative way, that Horace was given two dollars to visit them and two more to return, Mr. Davenport chastises the boy: "You're a grown man. Aren't you ashamed to take money from your mama? When I was your age, I had been supporting my mother and my brothers and sisters for eight years. Nobody ever gave me anything and I never asked for anything. What kind of man are you gonna make, taking money from a woman at your age?" Pete's narcissism and sexism drive Horace from the room, leaving Corella with "a splitting headache." Later Will, with all the enthusiasm of a gentleman caller, wants to show Horace and, more important, Pete how he and Lily Dale can waltz like "the Texas Castles: Irene and Vernon." When Lily responds that she has a similar "headache," Will insists, forcing her to dance a few steps. The underlying tension over the intruder pains both women. They know Horace is not welcome, but they are powerless to change things.[10]

Horace is seized by a mysterious fever at the end of Act I. When he faints, the others fear he has malaria and describe him as near death, out of his head, and unable to communicate for a week. Once he regains consciousness, Lily Dale reports to Horace that, during the two-week attack, "You thought Mr. Davenport had a butcher knife and was trying to kill you. You kept screaming, 'He's trying to slit my throat. Don't let him slit my throat.' Mrs. Westheimer heard you all the way upstairs and thought

10. Ibid., 192–93, 222.

we were being murdered and made Mr. Westheimer go for the police."[11] Although the hysteria of the scene is somewhat comical, Foote's point is serious. Horace's fever is a symptom of his fear and rage, directed consciously toward Pete Davenport and subconsciously toward the boy's mother and sister.

Following his fever Horace becomes obsessed with whether he has been baptized. He feels "dirty" and desires "to be washed clean." The literal explanation he offers is his recollection of Mrs. Coons, a Baptist lady on the train who warned that he should worry about "the wrath of my God," get a Bible, and inquire about his baptism. But Horton Foote's God is not the wrathful one this woman worships, and baptism is not the real issue. Like Flannery O'Connor, Foote uses this obnoxious evangelical to remind Horace of the love and grace which is his religious heritage. Not unlike Mrs. Tillman in *The Traveling Lady,* Mrs. Coons ministers to Horace, even if her message is off-key. Seeing Horace's confusion, she offers a benediction: "Father, I've been asked to remember in my prayers this young man, Horace, and his dear mother, Corella, and his dear sister, Lily Dale. Father of mercy, Father of goodness, Father of forgiveness. . . ." Like the later play *Dividing the Estate, Lily Dale* ends with a prayer for those who have lost their way.[12]

The nature of this loss is expressed in Lily Dale's everyday dreams, as well as in Horace's feverish ones. Horace's sister has a recurrent nightmare about being "kidnapped and they won't let me go until I'm an old woman, and I come home and no one recognizes me." With no emotional or spiritual home, she fears the life process; she lives an unrecognized existence and has no identity. And so she drifts toward Will Kidder and the false security provided by new homes and other material possessions. Although Horace wants to remember their father's words and reminds his sister of the song after which she was named, Lily Dale flees the past and fantasizes about "happy times, pleasant things." Her faith lies in an imaginary time when children will not know about "drunkards and dying and not having enough to eat." Lily Dale lives in a narcissistic fog, imagining herself as a famous pianist while her brother is buried with their father. She also fantasizes causing Will to die of a broken heart. Denying the truth of history

11. Ibid., 204.
12. Ibid., 208, 174, 250.

and the joy of dancing, Lily Dale becomes, in the words of her own song, a "poor, lost Lily Dale," a "Lily Rag" dedicated to herself.[13]

As much as *Lily Dale* is about paralysis, *The Widow Claire* is about transition. When Horace's sister calls "Oh, Brother! Brother! . . . let's be close," she really has only herself in mind. Intimacy to her is identified with being able to come to Horace "with my troubles"; it is a one-way proposition. Horace finds a similar woman in Widow Claire, who in Act I says her "motto" is "Don't look back . . . look ahead."[14] Like Lily, Claire indulges herself in adolescent behavior, entertaining her gentleman friends and often ignoring her children's warnings and fears. Her character not only recalls Lily Dale, but also anticipates Elizabeth Vaughn. Claire wants to mark her husband's life by putting a tombstone on his grave, she is sensitive to others, and she wants to give the children a picture so they will remember her. She does not always live for the future, despite her motto.

Of the nine *Orphans' Home* plays, *The Widow Claire* is the least focused on Horace's search for a home. Instead, it expands and qualifies Foote's primary themes by studying human sexuality. Although Claire respects and befriends Horace, she is attracted to Val, who is more aggressive, even violent. Whereas a play like *Blind Date* celebrates the free expression of the female psyche, here Claire resents her lost freedom and accepts the abusive Val into her home late at night. As a result, Horace is given the chance to observe the erotic and even masochistic impulses in some women before he pursues his healthier relationship with Elizabeth Vaughn.

In *The Widow Claire*'s exploration of physical desire there is talk of the "other kind" of girl as well as references to frigidity, getting the kids out the way, and stealing kisses. Still an innocent—"nice" and "sweet" as Claire calls him—Horace needs these experiences to move toward goodness rather than simple sweetness.[15] In his pursuit of a family, there is still something wounded and childlike about Horace; he needs to learn about passion before he can become committed. The dark sexuality of *The Widow Claire* is part of his education.

As he discovers the unsettling and mysterious nature of sex, Horace also learns the value of friendship. Like Mrs. Watts and Thelma in *The Trip*

13. Ibid., 179, 231, 201, 236–37, 231, 242, 205.
14. Ibid., 217, 279.
15. Ibid., 306, 287.

to Bountiful, Horace and Claire find each other at night and meet each other's immediate needs. Claire gains an image of commitment, rootedness, family, and love. She consequently finds the courage to give up Val, move to Galveston, and marry Ned. Although Horace observes the joys and insecurities of genuine passion, he and Claire cannot stay together: their chemistry and timing are wrong. She respects but does not desire him, and he needs peace and order rather than adventure. They serve each other best by following Claire's declaration, "It's been very nice knowing you, and the children and I wish you a lot of luck."[16]

Usually a playwright of family virtues and order, Horton Foote shows his respect for ambiguity and change in *The Widow Claire.* In this play human beings, especially women, are not judged against any standard of morality, even the writer's own. Horace does not condemn Claire for her promiscuity, or try to possess her. He recognizes her loneliness, and he enjoys their brief friendship. In *The Widow Claire* Foote acknowledges that certain transitory relationships are necessary and valuable, and that an erotic dimension is integral to human affairs. Rootedness and tradition remain the goals of Foote's best, most moral people, but in *Widow Claire* he acknowledges that mutability is more present than order. Peace and contentment are the goals of his characters, but they also must embrace and sometimes even celebrate change.

The erotic impulses so powerfully expressed in *Widow Claire* are given shape and direction in *Courtship.* Here Foote's imagination integrates two of his central metaphors: the cycle of nature, which is the province of God, and the dance, man's most resonant form of expression. This play is Foote's most sensual as well as his most romantic because, like the dancers described in the play, Horace and Elizabeth are drawn together by the powerful need for closeness. But Horace has learned, as has Elizabeth, that intimacy also has rules. In *Courtship* they test their desire against certain conventions; some they break, others they decide to obey. Their love gives them the courage to do both.

Courtship, like many of Foote's dramas, explores the relationship between death and desire. The aunts discuss the many deaths, often by suicide, that have occurred. Elizabeth's previous beau has died, and Sybil Thomas dies in childbirth during the play. Repeatedly confronted with the

16. Ibid., 330.

fragility of human existence, many characters feel a deeper hunger for life—a hunger often expressed as sexual desire. Horace and Elizabeth are energized by this passion: Elizabeth: "Why are boys so wild?" / Horace: "Girls can be wild, too."[17] Desire, diffuse and verging on the chaotic in *The Widow Claire,* becomes ordered by the powerful intimacy of the two lovers in *Courtship.* The social and sexual risks of their involvement, however, are not ignored. Their wildness is counterpointed with references to elopement, illegitimate births, shotgun weddings, and abortion, a point not lost on Mrs. Vaughn, who warns the children, "Well, think about poor Sybil Thomas the next time you start slipping around with boys in a buggy in the middle of the night." The adults are not alone in their fears of freedom and experimentation. Near the end of the play's long night, Laura's spell of worry leads her to ask her older sister, "Could what happened to Sybil Thomas ever happen to you? I don't mean the dying part. I know we all have to die. I mean the other part . . . having a baby before she was married."[18] *Courtship* is about the power of sexuality, the risks it demands, the fear it engenders, and the opportunities it offers, especially for women.

By welcoming Horace's love—both his sweetness and his wildness—Elizabeth is given the chance to decide, to risk her life and thus gain it. Laura's anxiety once again clarifies the issue:

Laura. Horace Robedaux is wild and you're attracted to him.
Elizabeth. I told you, I don't think he's so wild. I certainly don't think he's as wild as they all make out.
Laura. I would be afraid of marrying a wild boy. They don't ever stay home and they drink and gamble and get into debt and neglect you and you die of a broken heart. Anyway, that's what Mama says.
Elizabeth. But if you don't marry someone you love . . . What then?

Despite the power of her father and the manipulation of her mother—and even her own uncertainty—Elizabeth decides to act. *Courtship* is about her courage to choose. When she declares to her sister "I'm marrying Horace

17. Foote, *Three Plays,* 20.
18. Ibid., 35, 42.

Robedaux," she moves toward autonomy and identity, the goals cherished by Foote's women.[19]

Like *Only the Heart, Courtship* is about respecting and at the same time transforming history. Elizabeth loves her parents and even finds strength in them; she is a Vaughn. But she cannot afford to be nostalgic or sentimental over her parents' world, for it lacks the passion and imagination she needs. By reclaiming the past, Elizabeth becomes capable of establishing an identity—an accomplishment unknown to Lily Dale. But it takes an act of personal courage—committing to marriage—for that identity to be made real.

Elizabeth's strength is realized when she crosses the threshold separating the Vaughn house from the rest of the community. This kind of transition is generally risky in Foote's imaginary worlds because a stable home is such a powerful source of order. When Brother Vaughn, for example, leaves that same house, he easily falls victim to temptation, unable to live outside the shadow of his father. Elizabeth pays a different price; she is orphaned by her actions. Once her parents cut off their communication, Elizabeth and Horace must make a rented room their first home, and cross yet another threshold to seek their own place of order and meaning.

This new place, their apartment in the house of the Pate family, is the implied subject of the next play, *Valentine's Day*. It is surrounded by all the images of chaos and self-destruction noted in Henry Vaughn's warnings to his daughter. Among the visitors at the apartment are Bobby Pate, who clings to his mother and his drunken monologues, and Miss Ruth Amos, who continually pursues Bobby in the romantic and pathetic hope that he will reform. George Tyler is addled and confused about his past and present realities, remembering that he loved his cousin and once attacked his wife with a knife. Though his son, Steve, follows his father around town, apologizing for and picking up after him, eventually the elder Tyler commits suicide. Such rampant disorder reminds Elizabeth of the death of her baby sister, Jenny.

But the home established by Elizabeth and Horace provides a refuge for their neighbors, like Bessie Steelmon and the Tylers, who continually return to the rented room for direction and clarification. There Bessie tells the truth about her parents, Steve explains his father's senseless cash gifts

19. Ibid., 7–8, 49.

to blacks and Horace at Christmas, and the bet between Brother and Bobby is revealed. Henry finally admits to the couple, "There's peace in this room and contentment. That's why I like to come here, I think. I said to Mrs. Vaughn, 'They don't have much but they're contented. You feel that.'"[20] The intimacy between Horace and Elizabeth is a powerful presence in their home; it gives order to their lives and those around them.

As in *The Habitation of Dragons* and other Foote plays, this spirit of intimacy makes forgiveness possible in *Valentine's Day*. The town, including the Baptist preacher, hopes for reconciliation between parents and children. Similarly, Horace asks Elizabeth to forgive his jealousy of her father's prestige. George Tyler wants to ask Horace to forgive him for being in love with Aunt Mary. And Henry Vaughn asks God to forgive the estrangement he feels toward Brother. They want, they say in passing, to forgive each other as God first forgave them; as Elizabeth tells Bobby Pate near the end of the play, "Everybody has forgiven everybody now."[21]

Consequently, *Valentine's Day* is not about the past elopement to which the title refers; like *Tomorrow* and other Foote plays, it is a Christmas story. The first two scenes take place on Christmas Eve and morning; the characters exchange presents, mention the birth of the baby (who will die in infancy), and call reconciliation "the nicest Christmas present of all."[22] Only half aware of the religious implications, the Harrisonians judge themselves by the ideal of the day; they sense perfection and their faltering attempts to reach it. Just as Horace wants a physical home, all the characters long for the contentment of a happy family and a love which brings peace.

Increasingly confused by the changes in Harrison, the people in *Valentine's Day* feel like orphans. What they want, what they hear in the Bible stories, is the contentment found in intimacy. It is the order Horace has found with his wife: "I am no orphan, but I think of myself as an orphan, belonging to no one but you. . . . I tell you I've begun to know happiness for the first time in my life. I adore you. I worship you . . . and I thank you for marrying me." There are repeated instances of disorder in Harrison, including the story Bobby Pate tells at the end of the play, about a man who beats his son for dressing in his sister's clothes. The alternative to this

20. Ibid., 103.
21. Ibid., 57, 82, 85, 102–103.
22. Ibid., 81.

chaos, according to *Valentine's Day,* is the saving grace of the home Elizabeth plans; it will have "red roses, yellow roses, pink roses, sweetheart roses, and climbing roses."[23] Love will have its place.

True to life, resolve and peace are always tested, as they are in *1918.* The seventh play is about World War I and the flu epidemic, forces of disintegration outside and within Harrison. More than any of the previous stories, it studies how people handle loss and grief. It reflects Horace's simple question, "How can human beings stand all that comes to them? How can they?"[24] Foote offers various answers; some are personal and some are social. Others are the rewards of religious acceptance of the spirit of love and the mystery of the human condition.

Like the two plays just discussed, *1918* celebrates the female spirit. The men are, the play implies, deeply sensitive: for example, Mr. Vaughn, nearly hysterical over Brother, desperately wants war (against the wishes of the rest of his family), and Horace does not want to take money from Mr. Vaughn for a new house—Elizabeth guesses he is too proud. But it is the women who understand these feelings and needs, not the men:

> *Elizabeth.* Horace felt since he was poor and had nothing . . . Oh, I really don't know how to explain it to you. It was pride, I guess, Mama.
> *Mrs. Vaughn.* Don't bother to explain it to me. I didn't think anything about it. I'm just explaining how sensitive your father is. He thought Horace still held a grudge against him because he wouldn't speak to you after your marriage.
> *Elizabeth.* Horace has never felt any grudge.
> *Mrs. Vaughn.* I know that. I'm just trying to explain how sensitive your father is, that's all.[25]

The emotional life of the family, and the community, are in the hands of the women. Elizabeth, however, is not without her doubts. The loss of her child to influenza fills her with superstition. She fears that God took Jenny

23. Ibid., 83, 107.
24. Ibid., 136.
25. Ibid., 130.

because Elizabeth had named the child after Elizabeth's own dead sister. And she is bitter and anxious about her inability to submit to God's will, as she confesses to Bessie: "I don't want this baby. I want my other baby back. I want Jenny back. I don't want this baby at all. [Pause.] And I'm afraid of ever saying that and thinking that. Afraid I'll be punished for not submitting to God's will in all this." Even Elizabeth is tempted by grief and wants immediate release from the pain of loss.[26]

Humming "Narcissus" to herself, Elizabeth is tempted to turn inward and despair over her losses. She would not be the only one; as Mrs. Vaughn remembers, the Steelmons were among the few who sent flowers to Jenny's funeral: "They sent flowers to the funeral. One of the few families that did. Everybody was so busy thinking about their own dead they didn't have time to worry with anyone else's grief."[27] Ideally, guilt and grief are shared by everyone in Harrison. If Elizabeth and the others give in to their temptation, the subsequent isolation will be destructive to the whole town, not just her. The community, when it is healthy, admits loss and reminds the bereaved that he or she is not alone.

Unfortunately, many Harrisonians repress their fear and anger until the emotions possess them. Unable to share their grief, they imagine a vengeful, punishing God such as the one created by Mrs. Coon Ferguson at the funeral of one of the Vaughn children. As Mrs. Vaughn remembers, "When we lost our second child your papa was sitting in the living room by her little coffin. Mrs. Coon Ferguson came into the room and said, 'Mr. Vaughn, did you ever think the death of this child was a judgment on you for not joining the church?' And his face flushed crimson, but he just said very quietly, 'No, Mrs. Ferguson, I never did.' "[28] In *1918* Mr. Vaughn's revulsion is indicative of the struggle within the community to make love—and the intimacy it engenders—the central value.

The writer's answer in the subtext of *1918* is a radical faith that finds peace even in the face of death. The angry, vengeful God of Calvinism is replaced by an endlessly loving one—as imagined by Mary Baker Eddy—who calls his children home. In the words of the hymn sung at the end of the play, "Oh, the peace of God be near us, / Fill within our hearts Thy

26. Ibid., 166, 163.
27. Ibid., 159.
28. Ibid., 151.

home / With thy bright appearing cheer us / In Thy blessed freedom come."[29] A benevolent God of love, peace, and order leads the characters beyond themselves. Personal grief is transformed into a call for intimacy, and the God of judgment is reborn as the God of mystery, offering the path and the personal understanding of the Christian stories as imagined by Horton Foote in *1918*.

In *Cousins* this image of community becomes the moral norm. Most of the humor comes from the family's bumping into relatives; everyone seems to be a cousin. As Gordon Kirby, one of Horace's many cousins, puts it, "We are kin to a lot of people, Cousin Horace."[30] The serious side to the issue examines the extent to which the characters are connected with others and thus feel kinship. In *Cousins* people who are obsessed with themselves become neurasthenic, while those who pursue the ideal of community can rest, assured of their intimacy with others.

When Horace visits his mother and sister, he finds them disabled by psychosomatic symptoms. As Will, Lily Dale's husband, explains to Horace, "between Lily Dale and your mama, they know every doctor in Houston, and as you know, your mama wasn't at all satisfied with her last two operations and Lily Dale has had two herself, not counting the Caesarian for the baby." Lily and her mother are full of worry, "delicate" and in "very poor health." Lily Dale still gets "her headaches."[31] And she, Will, and Lola seek out fortune-tellers. Unable to establish loving attitudes and empathy with others, they have little personal peace. They have flattened religious experience into an endless search for a physical, external sense of security.

They represent the mid-1920s and the ever-present emphasis in the United States on upward mobility, with the accompanying materialism and loss of the past. Will and Lily Dale sell their two Packards to feel alive. As Will explains, he has "the Midas touch. Everything I touch makes money."[32] In the process they lose fellow-feeling and the recognition of their ties to and responsibility toward others, signified by Monty's denial of his kinship to Mae Buchanan. He would rather have wealth and feelings of superiority. The desire for money and external power, the obsessive need to get ahead, has alienated the characters from their natural cousins.

29. Ibid., 176.
30. Foote, *Two Plays,* 6.
31. Ibid., 31, 38, 44, 86.
32. Ibid., 31.

At the other extreme is Horace, who trades with blacks even though it hurts his business, because he believes in the dignity of all people. He is committed to his place and community. Ironically, his connection with others, past and present, frees him from personal guilt and repression. When Lola wants to know of the old feuds, especially about Horace's family being cheated out of money, he replies, "But that's all past and what can you do about it?"[33] While Lily Dale lives for the future and has bitter memories of the past, Horace has made his peace with the past so he can live in the present for others.

Cousins is also about recognizing the family as a metaphor for the sense of human community, threatened by modern American life. Because life is about endless change, centrifugal forces will destroy the center of things unless the Foote characters commit to the communal life. As Minnie Robedaux explains, "A family is a remarkable thing, isn't it? You belong. And then you don't. It passes you by. Unless you start a family of your own."[34] This sense of generation is at the heart of *Cousins*. Without the image of community and the commitment to life with others, lived with empathy and love, the center will not hold.

With *The Death of Papa* the story of Horace Robedaux in many ways comes full circle. This play ends with the death of Henry Vaughn, just as *Roots in a Parched Ground* began with the death of Paul Horace. There is the same conflict between the Robedaux love of books and the more active life of the Thorntons. Brother's rootlessness, which mirrors Horace's early condition, is contrasted with the home Elizabeth and Horace have found together. And Horace Jr.'s introduction to injustice, racism, alcoholism, deception, and death parallels Horace's own fall from innocence in the first four stories. Appropriately, in a cycle about going away and coming home, generation, and the eternal return, Horace arrives where he departed.

There are some significant shifts in emphasis, however, in the final play in the cycle. Here African Americans, with a deep intuitiveness about life, help to interpret the emotional lives of the other characters. For example, Gertrude explains to Elizabeth that Horace Jr. is too young to fully understand the death of his grandfather. And there is a deeper sense of racial difference and obligations in this last play. Gertrude tells why she goes to

33. Ibid., 61.
34. Ibid., 92.

84

school: "To help our race." Later, when Horace Jr. asks what he can do to help his race, his mother answers, "Start by being a good man; that will help all the races." And Brother is even more rootless after the death of his father, reacting with self-pity to Horace's good home: "I used to feel so sorry for you when you would come and call on Elizabeth. I'd hear Papa and Mama talking and they said you were practically an orphan and had no home. Now you have a home and I don't."[35]

Horace's home, the envy of Brother, is more than a physical space; it is a process of education and self-discovery. Like Mrs. Vaughn, Horace first had to learn that "we have to go on, you know. On and on and on." And then, although it takes some time, he experiences the truth of Mrs. Vaughn's words to Horace Jr., "Grief makes us so selfish," enabling him to offer a degree of forgiveness and gain some resolution. Horace is able to revise his history, to remythologize the past, in order to live more vitally with others: "I only know when I got into trouble there was no one I could turn to to help me out. . . . There was a time I felt very bitter about it. I felt no one cared about me at all. Now I don't know."[36] Although he is still wounded, Horace's intimate life with Elizabeth has helped him find the courage to face his past. In the spirit of forgiveness he is ready to live and die.

The Orphans' Home began under the most personal of circumstances. The death of Horton Foote's parents inspired him to write his most ambitious study of memory, loss, and change. He began with a social and moral history of Wharton, Texas, in the first three decades of the twentieth century, a story dedicated to the memory of Albert Horton and Hallie Brooks Foote. As much as the requirements of his form and imagination would allow, he was true to that story, but the cycle that grew from Foote's personal experience is about change in all places and times. *The Orphans' Home* studies courage as essential to sane, benign, and peaceful life, and like his other works, it discovers how the power of intimacy makes all this possible. It imagines everyone as an orphan looking for a home.

35. Ibid., 105, 115, 149, 194.
36. Ibid., 192, 140, 181.

7

Tender Mercies

The coherent vision that informs Horton Foote's writing is most obvious in his personal work, but it is also present in his commissioned work, his "writing for hire," as he likes to call it. His creative obsession with confusion, disorder, suffering, and loss—all of which follow unavoidable change—is present not only in *The Chase* and *The Trip to Bountiful* but also extends to, among others, *The Shape of the River, The Shadow of Willie Greer, Old Man,* and *Displaced Person.* In all these works the characters' courage is tested. Each must face and accept his past, recognize his wounds and burdens, and assume the responsibility for his future. There is no other path to health and peace in Foote's imaginative world.

The previous chapter examined the Foote vision in his most autobiographical work; this chapter also focuses on a specific case, but one substantially different from *The Orphans' Home.* A single work rather than a cycle, *Tender Mercies* was from its inception a much less personal work. Foote needed money to support himself and his family while he was trying to get *Orphans* produced. He approached his agent with a story about aspiring young musicians—though Foote had little knowledge of the music business. Unlike most of his work, *Tender Mercies* began as a relatively calculated effort, which Foote based on secondhand information. It had little of the compulsive need that had inspired *The Orphans' Home*.[1]

Ironically, the collaborative nature of moviemaking led Foote back to his personal vision. With each description, treatment, or draft he moved closer to his own preoccupations. A story of adolescent rebellion evolved into a study comparing youth with maturity. And then a love story emerged, only to transform itself into a search for family and identity. Of course, some Foote material needed to be reduced, and some eliminated, in the interest of economy of storytelling on film. The visual needs of the medium were met, and the filmmakers for the most part understood and respected the writer's vision. And so the making of *Tender Mercies* encouraged the development of "The Singer and the Song" (a working title for the first draft) into another Foote story.[2]

Foote at first imagined a movie based on the problems faced by his nephew as a member of a country and western band. Before writing a word, Foote took the idea to Lucy Kroll, his agent. She not only liked the idea; she felt the writer should go to Hollywood and try to sell the industry on the concept. Shy about such salesmanship and allergic to the film establishment, Foote initially balked at the plan. But Kroll persisted and he eventually, though reluctantly, agreed and flew to Los Angeles.[3]

Still without a written treatment, he met with producers at Twentieth Century Fox, where at first he was lucky. The success of *Breaking Away* had predisposed Hollywood to another youth-oriented movie. They liked Foote's story of young musicians who face poverty, rejection, and family problems but eventually find success. Though one executive suggested the story needed an older man to complement the young men's experiences, the company agreed to the concept. Foote was to return to New York and send Lucy Kroll back west to finish the deal. The package seemed complete.[4]

But the second trip to Hollywood was not as lucky as the first. When Ms. Kroll arrived in Los Angeles, she read in the industry paper of a major shakeup at Fox. All the people who had agreed to the Foote project had

1. Wood and Barr, " 'Certain Kind of Writer,' " 230.
2. MS in Foote Papers.
3. Wood and Barr, " 'Certain Kind of Writer,' " 230; Horton Foote, interview with author, March 15, 1988.
4. Foote interview.

left the company. And, as she knew would happen, the new leaders at the studio had deals of their own. The earth had moved again in California. Foote certainly had no deal, and apparently there was no interest in this film. Overnight his idea was dead in the water. And he still had no treatment, and no screenplay, not even in drafts or fragments.[5]

But Foote always has been resilient and persistent. By the time the deal had fallen through, the story had begun to intrigue him. So he decided to write it for himself. Remembering the suggestion at Fox that he include a contrasting older person, Foote created the Mac Sledge character: "I began thinking about this older person. So I wrote *Tender Mercies* on my own; I didn't have any . . . help from a studio. And whatever happens to your imagination, he became quite interesting to me." In Foote's first notes for "The Singer and the Song," Mac enters before the boys in the band; early in the treatment his story is integrated with theirs. Rosa Lee is there, though she and Mac are not linked romantically until Mac's problems with Dixie are well developed. Foote had not as yet focused on the Mac/Rosa Lee/Sonny triad.[6]

With the first draft of the film, the writer settled on the title *Tender Mercies,* which he had written as an alternative title in his original notes for "The Singer and the Song." The piece had become a pastoral story, focusing on Rosa Lee's home, gardening, and work on the land. The early drafts tell a complicated story, including a trip to a drive-in movie, a visit to the parents of Rosa Lee's dead husband, and fights between Dixie and Sue Anne. Sue Anne is portrayed as an ambitious singer; she and her boyfriend seek an audition with the band. Mac sings the dove song down along the river, and the film ends with geese flying to the Gulf. It is a coastal southeast Texas story equally attentive to Mac and the band.[7]

In one early version the screenwriter even employed flashbacks, remembering that director Bruce Beresford used them in his Australian films. But Beresford and his editor, William Anderson, were more concerned with dramatic structure than film technique. Beresford had great respect for the writer's dialogue and character development, but he felt the

5. Lucy Kroll, interview with author, June 5, 1990; Wood and Barr, " 'Certain Kind of Writer,' " 230; Foote interview.

6. Wood and Barr, " 'Certain Kind of Writer,' " 230, and MS in Foote Papers.

7. Ibid.

screenplay was too diffuse. It needed economy—in place, plot, characters, and theme. As the revisions demonstrate, the process of shooting helped the story refocus on Mac and his relationships with Rosa Lee and Sonny. The needs of the filmmakers called for the screenplay to concentrate on the family, which was not a characteristic of the early drafts.[8]

In *Tender Mercies* collaboration actually helped Horton Foote return to his instincts as a writer. Robert Duvall, Brad Wilson (Duvall's assistant), and EMI added a musical score which, except for the final song, gave appropriate highlights and nuances to the script. The grandparents (though initially included in the shooting) were dropped, as was a sexual relationship between Harry and Dixie, Sue Anne's career and interest in the band, and Menefee (Sue Anne's boyfriend), except for the brief shot of him in a car. As the Hobels (the producers), Beresford, and Anderson pushed for economy, Dixie became a less complex, more negative character, and Rosa Lee's confusion was minimized, as was her interest in singing. It became another Foote study in the transformative power of intimacy and responsibility.[9]

This collaboration resulted in a final shooting script remarkably similar in theme and structure to *The Orphans' Home*. *Tender Mercies*, like the cycle, begins with the breakup of one family and moves to the creation of a stronger, more nurturing one. Just as Horace, in *Roots in a Parched Ground*, faces the chaos following the death of his father and the remarriage of his mother, Mac struggles with the end of his two marriages, estrangement from his daughter, and alcoholism. Horace courts Elizabeth Vaughn; Mac finds Rosa Lee. For both men marriage is healing. They share their wounds with their wives, who listen attentively, understand, and help the men draw supportive boundaries. Sustained by such attachments, Horace and Mac find the strength to face death—of a father-in-law and a daughter—without despair. They have found themselves and thus are ready to die peacefully, not tragically.

This strength and transcendence relies on the men's sense of place. Their wives are certainly the rocks upon which they are able to recover their stability. But Mac, no less than Horace, moves beyond that one at-

<hr>

8. Ibid; Foote interview; Bruce Beresford to author, February 6, 1989.
9. Philip and Mary-Ann Hobel, interview with author, September 27, 1990; Robert Duvall, telephone interview with author, December 16, 1993; and MS in Foote Papers.

tachment. Like Foote's other healthy men, the singer grows from one intimacy to another; his roots give him wings. Mac's growth is realized when he sluggishly opens up to Sue Anne and when he passes a football with Sonny after confessing his own lack of trust. Less obviously, Mac connects with the local community through his baptism. He does not profess his faith in a doctrinal fashion, but as a commitment to a tradition that includes his wife and those before her. As he reduces his personal confusion, he is drawn outside of himself to the communities, secular and religious, which surround him. Like Horace, he finds more than one home.

But it is Sonny, not Mac, who is most like Horace in his quest for a lost father. Horace is paralyzed in *Convicts* by his conflicting hunger for a father and his revulsion at Soll's violent racism. Horace eventually resolves his ambivalence when he makes peace with Henry Vaughn, respecting the patriarch's power and grace while recognizing the older man's lack of empathy and flexibility. Sonny's conflict with Mac is similar, though less profound. At first suspicious of the singer, fearing that Mac will come between him and his mother, Sonny tosses stones at him. After the marriage, however, he defends his stepfather on the playground and later declares his affection for Mac at the dance hall. His search for the truth about his biological father parallels his growing attachment to Mac Sledge.

The darkness in *Tender Mercies* is also similar to that in *The Orphans' Home,* for both dramatize how certain forces often make healing attachments ineffective or, in some cases, impossible. Menefee's alcoholism and three failed marriages are uncomfortable parallels to Mac's history. Drugs in the schools, like alcohol at the dance hall, are a negative reality, and death is as real as love, arriving with the impersonality of war or the suddenness of an automobile accident. Ultimately, time is the final antagonist, for Mac loses his chance to call Sue Anne "Sister" and his need for healing will never end. He is, for the rest of his days, an alcoholic.

In *Tender Mercies,* as in *The Orphans' Home,* the most effective barriers to intimacy are not physical but psychological. One of these is narcissism. In *Orphans* Horace needs more than Elizabeth to stop his pain. He must resolve his feelings of betrayal and abandonment toward his parents, especially his mother. By choosing to follow her new husband and the security he offers, she commits a most primitive act of emotional violence. Though he rarely mentions his hurt, Horace's rage over this rejection is the source of his sickness in *Lily Dale.* Only late in the cycle is he able to revise his view, the first step toward forgiving his mother. By letting go of this anger, Horace reduces his self-absorption, thus freeing him to empathize with others and act more selflessly.

This theme is even more integral to *Tender Mercies* than to *The Orphans' Home*. Dixie repeatedly imagines that Mac is jealous of her success or vengeful over her lack of support for his songs. Only able to see the world as a reflection of her hurts and needs, she lives a distorted and painful existence. Mac has a similar childlike quality throughout the story. He tends to react to pain with rage and repeatedly withdraws from Rosa Lee, his source of understanding and support. Violence and self-destruction become possible because he turns too far inward. By the end of the drama, however, he is better able to share his emotional life, to (in his words) tell Rosa Lee everything about himself. Once he admits his confusion, as he does in the final garden scene, he is able to move toward Sonny and share a life beyond his own.

As is typical of Foote's work, women are the most centered and least narcissistic of the characters. In *The Orphans' Home* Elizabeth Vaughn finds the courage to rebel against her father, the most powerful man in town, in order to marry Horace. Unconcerned with her own safety, and certainly less fearful than Laura, Elizabeth is able to minister to Horace, the needier one. Similarly, though with less self-understanding, Rosa Lee is strengthened by her religion, which asks her to follow a path not hers but God's. She embraces the mystery which Mac fights and is consequently less concerned for herself. More accepting of the nature of things, of God's universe, Rosa Lee is able to love with less fear.

The garden scene near the end of *Tender Mercies* provides a good example. At first viewing, it seems tragic; Mac declares to Rosa Lee that he does not know why he survived an automobile accident while his daughter did not. His words appear as the heartfelt expression of an otherwise emotionally insulated man. But Rosa Lee has a strong presence throughout the scene; she is a witness to his pain, although she offers no palliative. By giving no explanations, even her own religious ones, Rosa Lee asks Mac to confront the limitations of his will in the face of the essential muddle of human experience. And Mac responds to Rosa Lee's instructive silence. Though he is becoming a good Baptist, Mac has discovered—like a good Catholic—that there is no grace in despair, no mercy for those who fail to love the mystery of human experience. Despite his contention that God has not answered his questions, Mac has received—through Rosa Lee—an answer to his prayers. By admitting his inability to see everything clearly, to know exactly, and to have God fully revealed in history, Mac gains an acceptance which, though easily confused with passivity or accommodation, is a religious offering from wife to husband.

Even when the characters act lovingly, grief remains a great temptation in both *The Orphans' Home* and *Tender Mercies*. Horace, having had to deal with the loss of his parents, a child, and his father-in-law, could have anesthetized himself from the pain by denying history and surrounding himself with new homes and expensive cars, as his sister has done. As Mrs. May in Foote's early play *Ludie Brooks* explains, he could have crippled himself with grief's inwardness: "Grief can cripple and destroy and consume us, just as much as drunkardness or sin, and it's here on this livin' earth just as they are to tempt us, and how each of us meets our temptation is a matter for your heart and my heart."[10] But Horace's relationship with Elizabeth inspires him to approach grief courageously. He will not, like Lily Dale, believe his life special; he will not spend time and energy trying to delay, reduce, or avoid the end of things.

Mac is similarly tempted by his losses. His prayers following Sue Anne's death were met, he says, with silence: "I prayed last night to know why I lived and she died, but I got no answer to my prayers." That thought leads to other anxieties about why he was able to find Rosa Lee but Sonny's father had to die in the Vietnam War. Overwhelmed by accident, death, and even survivor's guilt, Mac is disoriented and confused: "I don't know the answer to nothing. Not a blessed thing."[11] Mac has lost his assurance; he feels alienated from meaning, purpose, from God. He stands, like the scarecrow beside him, a hollow shell blowing pointlessly in the wind.

Fortunately, the trust and commitment between Mac and Rosa Lee have established a safe place from which he can face his demons—reanimated by grief—without guilt, shame, or rejection. And thus he is able to control his inwardness and unconsciously explore his dark feelings. His terrifying descent into confusion finally teaches him that "I don't trust happiness. I never did, I never will."[12] A sad reality, this character flaw is

10. Horton Foote, *Ludie Brooks* [teleplay] for *Lamp unto My Feet*, February 4, 1951, p. 24 (MS in Foote Papers).

11. Horton Foote, *Tender Mercies*, in *Three Screenplays*, 144.

12. Ibid., 145.

the basis of the fearful disconnection that haunts his life. Once he has uncovered this truth, Mac is strengthened by his insight. Armed with this awareness, he is able to reach out to Sonny in the final shots of the movie. By discarding the stone of distrust, as well as the self-pity which accompanies it, Mac can recover his loving nature with Sonny, if not Sue Anne. Having tended his emotional garden, Mac makes his past his own.

In the process he reveals a better way than the one chosen by Dixie, Mac's ex-wife. In the previous scene Dixie has responded to their daughter's death by surrounding herself with nurses, medication, all the luxury of her possessions. Seeing only herself in the tragic drama, she cries, "Mac . . . why has God done this to me? Why has God done this to me?"[13] Unable to share her pain, she feels singled out by God for punishment. But Mac shares his feelings with Rosa Lee, the benevolent witness to his loss, and thus avoids Dixie's paralysis. As he moves closer to Rosa Lee, he grows more flexible and courageous.

As his examination of grief in *Tender Mercies* reveals, Foote's vision is never nostalgic. He often writes about the past, and his characters often hold values which are being questioned or undermined. But his stories have a hard edge of inevitable change. Death and violence are ever-present realities, as are the centrifugal forces of confusion and meaninglessness. If Foote's characters are fully honest with themselves, they are able to discover a profound insecurity at the heart of things. They share provisional lives; they have a common adversary—time—and similar feelings of deprivation and loss.

In the face of this very real darkness, Foote's "orphans," in *Tender Mercies* as elsewhere, find peace in loving families. In *Tomorrow* Fentry's love for Sarah leads him to adopt and protect her child. Although time does not offer him the opportunity, he plans to build a house in the woods and make a place for three people in the wilderness. Similarly, Mac Sledge— unfortunately poisoned by two failed marriages and the loss of his daughter—longs for a family that will offer him an identity, a sense of generation

---

13. Ibid., 144. See also the words of Leonard, a character in Foote's unproduced commissioned screenplay *A Christmas Story,* written in the late 1970s as he was completing *The Orphans' Home* and beginning *Tender Mercies:* "I swear Mary, sometimes I think money is a curse. If we didn't have money we couldn't indulge our grief. We would have to stay where we were and work it out. Not go running around here and there" (p. 38).

and tradition. Finding his place helps him to realize the courage to face his demons, love others, and prepare to die.

But the writer is not sentimental about families. He does not reduce life to blood ties or simple ceremonies. In *Tomorrow,* for example, the dark kinship of the Eubanks clan, with the authority of the law, drags Jackson and Longstreet from Fentry. The family becomes the excuse for and the instrument of betrayal and violence. Healthy families, like those imagined by Sarah and Fentry and by Rosa Lee and Mac, are offered as a graceful presence among many confusions, not unlike the sanctuary Foote creates in the "rented room" of Elizabeth and Horace Robedaux in *Valentine's Day.* The best families offer a healing sense of order.

But *Tender Mercies* is not only about the family. As Horton Foote has repeatedly explained, "If you have to say there is a theme to my work, it's . . . people's courage."[14] He writes to study why some people are able to face up to life's vagaries when others cannot. His three Faulkner adaptations, for example, explore this problem. The convict in *Old Man* is able to accept unjust reincarceration because his few days of love and meaningful work will sustain him. In *Barn Burning* Sarty's intelligence and love of justice inspire his betrayal of his father and blood ties. And in *Tomorrow* Fentry's ability to love, to be a husband and father, strengthens his opposition to natural and civil law.

Other sources of courage include memories of early loving attachments, for they can empower adult characters to face inevitable exigencies of time and change. *To Kill a Mockingbird,* for example, is a memory story in which Scout, the narrator, is strengthened by reminders of Atticus's integrity and responsibility. She remembers that fear, in the figure of Boo Radley, can be made a friend and that, following her father's example, she, too, can be courageous. And like Scout remembering her loving father, Will Mayfield in *The Death of the Old Man* takes strength from his history of investing "in livin' things."[15] In the face of despair, previous experiences of empathy and loyalty remain as a source of hope.

Horton Foote's characters, especially the males, are tempted to reduce courage to will or physical action. In *The Chase,* Sheriff Hawes undergoes a long transition, a kind of breakdown, in his way of seeing things that

14. Hachem, "Foote-Work," 40.
15. Foote, *Selected One-Acts,* 135.

begins with guilt over his violent past. With an almost paralyzing introspection, and with the substantial support of his wife, Hawes wants to rid himself of these violent impulses. During the play, and the novel Foote wrote from it, the sheriff learns to be less preoccupied with the public good and his own security. He chooses instead a life of conscience back on the farm. By abandoning the world of control and political influence, Hawes finds courage in personal conviction and purity of motive. It is an issue of the mind, not the body.

Not all Foote's characters find courage, of course. Harvey Weems in *The Midnight Caller* is defeated by alcohol, as is Horace Robedaux's father in *Roots in a Parched Ground*. And George Tyler of *On Valentine's Day*, like Annie Gayle Long of *Spring Dance*, can never face up to the reality of loss and failure. They lack essential attachments, or they resort to endless clinging, lost in suffocating ties that bind rather than liberate. Most parallel to Mac Sledge is Henry Thomas, from the play *The Traveling Lady* and its film version, *Baby, the Rain Must Fall*. A country and western singer, Henry has a loving wife who desperately wants a stable family, especially for their daughter, Margaret Rose. But Henry was orphaned too young and placed with the abusive, rejecting Kate Dawson. Intimacy, fidelity, and honesty are lost on Henry; he remains rootless and self-destructive.

The key to Mac's courage—what he has that Henry Thomas lacks—is a sense of place. Henry is unable to connect with his family, whereas Mac finds not just a physical home but an emotional and spiritual one as well. In his stumbling, fitful way Mac learns to share his burdens and finds that he cannot live a fulfilling life in isolation; he must make a place—with a wife, son, and satisfying work—where he is accepted and valued. There he learns to share his feelings and accept himself, even his distrust of happiness. With Rosa Lee's support, he even begins to gain a vision of a purposeful and merciful existence. In Foote's search for the sources and nature of courage, *Tender Mercies* reminds us that courage begins in healthy homes, whether rediscovered or established for the first time.

In *Tender Mercies* Horton Foote places this search for courage in a religious context unrecognized by the characters themselves. He transforms the indigenous southern Protestantism of rural Texas into a distinctive fictional world informed by the rituals of the High Church, the images of Catholicism, and his own Christian Science. For example, although they are largely unaware of the depths of their neediness, his characters are emotionally and spiritually, as well as physically, hungry. When characters like Mac, "guess" they "could eat something," their meals often become a form of communion. And water, whether in rain showers or a baptism, is there as a source of comfort. Best of all, there is love, a spirituality imagined in birds and Rosa Lee's madonna-like presence. Loving connections surround the "orphans," whether they know it or not, whether they believe it or not.

Despite the presence of these themes, *Tender Mercies* is not pure Foote. The writer was reluctant to give up, for example, the final image of geese flying to the Gulf; however, director Bruce Beresford convinced Foote that his ending would seem forced and would appear as a process shot in an otherwise natural-looking film. Besides, Foote was told, the film was made just south of Dallas, a place short on geese and a gulf. The writer was also disappointed that some well-acted scenes had to be dropped, to avoid redundancy, during editing.[16] In one, at the gravesite of their daughter, Dixie offered Mac forgiveness for his abuses during their marriage, revealing her pain and fitful desire for peace. Its omission makes Dixie more one-dimensional than most Foote women. Most of all, *Tender Mercies* is not the coastal southeast Texas film first imagined by the writer. Its landscape is a bit flat and barren, and its people look a bit too much like cowboys. They might have known Larry McMurtry.

The modifications in *Tender Mercies* were the result of many collaborations. Although the other artists respected Foote's writing, his words were sometimes changed; he added scenes and the actors occasionally improvised. Even more significant were the choices of location, set, and costuming. An east Texas story was moved to a central Texas that sometimes had the sound and feel of west Texas. The emphasis on open spaces, flat and sometimes forbidding landscapes grew naturally from Foote's interest in dislocated, orphaned Texans. But the details in the look of *Tender Mercies* are not his. Finally, the story was trimmed, and trimmed again, to focus on the creation of a family. The other characters, as the film was edited, became counterpoints for the essential drama of Mac, Sonny, and Rosa Lee.[17]

The story of the making of *Tender Mercies* is, in many ways, the story

16. Foote interview.
17. MS in Foote Papers.

of any film. The essentially visual nature of the medium forces the artists to move beyond the words, the "literature," of the writer. The choice of location and specific details of costuming and lighting create a look that has a life of its own, often separate from the intentions and original conceptions of the writer. Financial demands keep intruding. Nature sometimes refuses to cooperate or offers unexpected gifts. In the camera actors may have a mysterious quality, a sense of threat, or humor that was unforeseen. And talented artists have their own needs to contribute, express themselves, or have their way. When the editing starts, some things are missing and others have a new life. Excellent bits of acting have to be dropped for the good of the project; technical problems can require a different shot or angle. The original treatment, as was the case with *Tender Mercies,* then becomes another film, one that was never made. The final shooting script is tighter, more economical and more focused, but it is a new generation.

What distinguishes *Tender Mercies* from most other films is not the process; it is the integrity of the vision. Obviously there was an uncommon respect for the writer, a respect which extended from Robert Duvall and Tess Harper to the Hobels, Bruce Beresford, and Jeanine Oppewall. Respect, however, was not enough. The writer's vision *had* to be transformed as it moved from script to screen, and other talents, beliefs, and prejudices needed to be implemented. And, as the producers emphasize, sometimes the artists were just lucky. During the making of *Tender Mercies,* the continuity was maintained as the story became less Foote's and more that of his collaborators. Despite the many changes, compromises, and surprises, Foote's vision—even in translation—remains. It is a writer's film even though it is not wholly his.

After all the collaboration, and after all the political decisions were made, *Tender Mercies* remains a story about the struggle between peace and confusion, identity and alienation, order and chaos. Once again the primary need is for intimacy established and exemplified by healthy families. The marriage of Mac and Rosa Lee, like that of Horace and Elizabeth in *The Orphans' Home,* is a metaphor for the deep need for identity and community. Mac and Sonny dramatize that need, and Rosa Lee makes it real. Characters hunger for deep and nourishing roots to sustain their parched lives, and discover that these places are especially hard to find in times of dislocation, materialism, and narcissism. Without such places, characters drift toward despair and violence, but with roots they gain a degree of grace and peace. Most of all, the characters need these ties—to family, work, the land, a community or religion—to know who they are, to live with empathy, and finally to die alone.

The Young Man from Atlanta

The drama for which Horton Foote won the 1995 Pulitzer Prize at first seems quite different from the subjects of chapters 6 and 7. *The Young Man from Atlanta* presents a more recognizably theatrical world, echoing other plays and playwrights in its exploration of social and political themes. Compared with *The Orphans' Home* and *Tender Mercies, Young Man* has fewer "privileged moments"—to borrow a phrase from François Truffaut—or times when Foote explores language and character with seeming disregard for dramatic progression. Closer to *Laura Dennis,* his last play in the Signature Theatre Company's 1994–95 series, *The Young Man from Atlanta* employs a seemingly traditional structure. Its obvious use of mystery to nudge the reader/audience forward, its continual asking of "What happened and why?" is not the usual Foote method. But the playwright's use of conventional dramatic form in *Young Man* is deceptive, for once again he turns the formulas against themselves, exploring his more personal, psychological, and finally religious ends.

Unusual for a Foote work, *The Young Man from Atlanta* admits early on that it has literary and theatrical sources. Similar to the one-act *The One-Armed Man,* which revisits Flannery O'Connor's "A Good Man Is

Hard to Find," this play borrows from Arthur Miller and, more immediately, David Mamet; it could be a coastal southeast Texas version of *Death of a Salesman* or *Glengarry Glen Ross*. *Young Man* opens in the office of a small Houston company seized with the post–World War II love of youth, accountability, and retrenchment. With his usual sense of the historical moment, and like other socially aware American playwrights, Foote initially satirizes (in the figure of Will Kidder) the need to have "the best of everything. . . . The biggest and the best." Will's manic optimism is satisfied only if, as he declares to co-worker Tom Jackson, "I live in the best country in the world. I live in the best city. I have the finest wife a man could have, work for the best wholesale produce company." Like previous critics of American society, Foote exposes Will's inflexible desire to compete, portraying him as a man without an emotional home.[1]

But *The Young Man from Atlanta* is not content with imitating the satire of other playwrights. In its very first moments Foote deflects the play from social commentary by injecting a Pinteresque intruder, a mysterious outsider who insinuates himself into the vulnerable relationship between Lily Dale and Will Kidder. This unseen Atlantan and his questionable motives denaturalize the play's political content; menace creates a theatrical sense of disorder and suspense. Subsequently, like a detective/mystery story, *Young Man* asks a number of pressing questions. Did Bill Kidder commit suicide? If so, why? What was his relationship to Randy Carter? Was Bill religious? What does the young man from Atlanta want from Lily Dale and Will? Is Pete's great-nephew Carson telling the truth? Are his motives different from Randy Carter's? Why did Bill give $100,000 to his roommate?

Even as *Young Man* fitfully pursues these questions, the playwright betrays his dissatisfaction with the mystery story he has begun in the first scenes. The play has come too close to formula and metatheater, styles too dehumanized for Foote's taste. And so, within a few moments after the opening curtain, he begins his typical dedramatization of the subject—especially its political and artistic content—in search of a more personal and realistic theater. In the first scene, for example, Will sounds like the typical detective when he asks, "Why in the middle of the day in a lake in

1. Horton Foote, *The Young Man from Atlanta*, introduction by Horton Foote (New York, 1995), 2–3.

Florida out in deep, deep water if you can't swim." Before the tension can build, however, Will answers his own question, defusing the audience's expectations: "Everyone has their theories, and I appreciate their theories, but I'm a realist. I don't need theories. I know what happened. He committed suicide." The rest of the play takes its cue from this deflation, giving no definitive explanation of why the son died, and the various rationalizations, even the convincing ones, contradict each other.[2] By the last scene, *The Young Man from Atlanta* has generated more mystery than it has solved.

The most obvious reason for Foote's repeatedly deviating from genre—in this case the detective/mystery story—is his creative obsession with his characters' problems with intimacy. Despite the melodrama surrounding Bill's death in *The Young Man from Atlanta,* the play's focus is not on suicide but on Will's inability to connect lovingly with his son. The father eventually confesses that his indifference was born of narcissism: "I just think now I only wanted him to be like me, I never tried to understand what he was like. I never tried to find out what he would want to do, what he would want to talk about." Sadly, Will is not the only male who is "never close" to others.[3] Pete, ostensibly a loving husband and stepfather, apparently has been a womanizer, and Randy Carter and Carson both claim to need father figures. Like an Ingmar Bergman story, *The Young Man from Atlanta* is haunted by the loss of benign paternity.

This search for absent fathers is a symptom of a general breakdown in family order in the play. While Will cannot communicate with his wife about the death of their son, Lily Dale confides in Randy Carter, the young man from Atlanta, rather than her husband. Will shares his deepest understandings with Tom Jackson because "I feel like you're my son in many ways." Similarly, Pete and Lily Dale make the visitors from Atlanta—Carson and Randy—into images of the dead son.[4] According to *The Young Man from Atlanta,* intimacy—when it is unrealized in caring families—tends to exceed safe and faithful limits, bringing more emotional chaos, vulnerability, and eventually violence.

As in many of Horton Foote's other works, this confusion of primary

2. Ibid., 6.
3. Ibid, 105.
4. Ibid., 5, 10, 76, 103.

attachments becomes a basis of humor. Throughout the play Lily Dale is obsessed with the "Disappointment Club," a purported program of absenteeism designed by Houston blacks during the 1930s to cause stress—disappointment—in the white homes where they were employed. Even though Lily Dale never confirms the existence of such a campaign, she embellishes the story and believes that Eleanor Roosevelt was the plan's instigator. When Will quizzes her about the supposed conspiracy, Lily insists: "I know she was. Everybody in Houston knows she was. She just hated the South, you know. She took out all her personal unhappiness on the South."[5] By projecting her own unhappiness onto the wife of the Democratic president, Lily Dale justifies the aggressive Republicanism she shares with her husband. Her private confusions lead her toward comic, and potentially destructive, political views.

Integral to *The Young Man from Atlanta*'s study of intimacy is its focus on grief's temptations and opportunities. Early in the play Will and Lily Dale use their new possessions to insulate themselves from loss; Will hopes "this new house will help us get away from a lot of memories. To celebrate the new house I'm buying my wife a new car." Conversely, the loss of these luxuries following the greater loss of their son eventually brings the couple closer. Once he has resolved his anger toward his wife, Will begins to accept his age and health problems, give up his pride and bitterness, and see himself as "a simple man at heart" in need of meaningful work. For her part, as Lily Dale confronts her profound loneliness and shares it with her husband, she becomes more realistic about her son and his death. Their gains are expressed in a simple exchange of shared loss near the end of the play; Will admits "I want my son back, Lily Dale," and she responds, "I know. I know. So do I."[6]

The Young Man from Atlanta, despite its sensational subject matter, is indifferent to the causes of the son's suicide, focusing instead on the effects of grief on the marriage of Lily Dale and Will Kidder; she needs to be more realistic about dark motives, the play determines, less a girl who calls her husband "Daddy,"[7] and he needs to live with all the unanswered questions about his son's death, including his failure as a father. Both need to

5. Ibid., 24.
6. Ibid., 8, 11, 66, 105.
7. Ibid., 25.

shift from taking comfort in their possessions to finding support in shared loss. The central dramatic issue in *Young Man* is not the boy's sexual orientation or the motives of the young man from Atlanta, but whether Lily Dale and her husband can integrate mystery into their emotional lives and find peace in their marriage—in the face of death.

Thus, in *The Young Man from Atlanta,* Foote uses the conventions of the detective/mystery story as a backdrop for his continuing exploration of the power of intimacy, his most prevalent artistic concern. Social, psychological, and even moral questions are raised which are purposely never answered. And Foote suggests that art, in its truthfulness to life, best serves its readers and audiences by not giving false assurances disguised as "closure" in traditional dramatic formulas. In fact, wonder is gained by admitting that the "whys" are often unknowable and not a source of peace. Resilience and courage are acquired by leaving many things with God.

This understanding eludes Lily Dale throughout most of *The Young Man from Atlanta.* Her infantile, self-obsessed religion allows her to deny the dark realities of Bill's life, leaving her vulnerable to Randy Carter's machinations. Rather than deal honestly with loss, she protects herself with innocent piety: "Every time I feel blue over missing Bill, I call his friend and I ask him to tell me again about Bill and his prayers and he does so so sweetly." This innocence leaves Lily Dale speechless after Allie Clinton's baiting question: "Why did this good God let your son commit suicide?" Feeling powerless and lacking the individuation so essential to Foote's characters, Lily accepts the image of God as controlling and vindictive.[8]

But in *The Young Man from Atlanta*—as in Foote's unpublished novel written twenty-five years earlier, *The Days of Violence*—African American women offer an alternative theodicy, a moral norm for Horton Foote's work. In the novel, the housekeeper Bessie serves as both caretaker and visionary. Gifted with second sight, she offers a benediction over Harrison, declaring in the final words of the story that the ghost of Robedaux Harris is "at peace now" while Homer Barnes still wanders around "begging for forgiveness." Although African Americans do not have the last word in *Young Man,* they similarly embrace a radical and healing vision of God-as-Love. Clara, the present maid, says Lily Dale needs "Christian faith," and

8. Ibid., 30, 29.

HORTON FOOTE and the Theater of Intimacy

Etta Doris, the former cook, benignly remembers Bill as a good-looking, friendly boy who liked baseball. Her truth is simple: "Everything changes. The Lord giveth and he taketh away. . . . We're here today and gone tomorrow. Blessed be the name of the Lord."[9] In *Young Man,* as in *Days,* everything else is a mystery.

This sense of mystery is the key to the last scene of *The Young Man from Atlanta,* one of the most resonant in all of Foote's work. It begins in a clutter of information. The narrative speed is almost dizzying by Foote standards: the Disappointment Club is reprised, Will's illness continues, Pete moves disturbingly close to his nephew, and Lily Dale sees the young man from Atlanta once again. Lily Dale reports that Randy is waiting just outside the house, arguing for his innocence and Carson's jealousy. Then Will appears from the bedroom, admitting to having "lost my spirit." "Here I am," he says, "in the finest city in the greatest country in the world and I don't know where to turn. I'm whipped."[10] Lily Dale responds by confessing a brief assignation she and cousin Mary Cunningham had with two men some twenty years earlier. Although childlike, the confession nevertheless encourages Lily Dale to acknowledge her loneliness and need for comfort.

This ambiguity deepens as the scene and the play come to a close. *The Young Man from Atlanta* offers the hope of reconciliation through the growing intimacy between Lily Dale and Will. He controls his anger and lets go of his bitterness, deciding to "swallow my pride" and return—out of genuine need—to his job at the bank. When she offers to "help us out" by teaching music, his response is empathetic: "If you like. It might give you something to think about." And yet, even as they grow closer, the husband and wife conspire to avoid the whole truth. Just as Lily Dale begins to admit the implications of Randy's declaration that "he loved" Bill "and missed him," Will cuts her off, offering the unwarranted assurance that ends the play: "Everything will be all right." While Will holds Lily Dale with genuine affection as the curtain falls, the ending to *Young Man* is purposely inconclusive.[11]

9. Horton Foote, *The Days of Violence* (MS in Foote Papers), 329; Foote, *Young Man,* 50, 84.

10. Foote, *Young Man,* 102.

11. Ibid., 107, 110. This apparently loose, open-ended scene is typical of many Foote plays and screenplays, especially the later ones. As Foote develops as a writer, his characters

Most arresting is the tacit agreement between husband and wife to create mystery in the final moments of *The Young Man from Atlanta*. When Lily Dale asks Will if he thinks Pete has been unfaithful, Will says, "I don't know. Who knows about anything, Lily Dale?" The husband also refuses to speak to Randy: "there are things I'd have to ask him and I don't want to know the answers." Finally, as Will considers the reasons the son gave money to his roommate, he stops himself: "Whatever the reasons, I don't want to know. There was a Bill I knew and a Bill you knew and that's the only Bill I care to know about." Will Kidder, the self-described realist, in the end chooses uncertainty rather than the truth he admires. Having spent the whole play trying to introduce Lily Dale to realities about Randy Carter, the Disappointment Club, and their son, he finally embraces a peaceful future in which the past remains unclear.[12]

When Will and Lily Dale decide to remember "the only Bill" they "care to know," everything changes.[13] Their agreement, while colored by shared fantasy, is not wholly innocent; it is a creative act—like the play itself—which values life without reference to truthful causes or even morality. In its final moments *Young Man* imagines the human mind—even in twentieth-century material America—participating in its own heaven or hell. By refusing to label their son with deadly reductive and judgmental names—like "suicide" and "homosexual"—the parents no longer want truth in the literal sense. Whether Randy or Carson is the liar will not be clarified. Bill's religious beliefs, if any, will not be established. His anger toward his father and the hollow places in his emotional life—his despair—will never be explained away. By making peace with these unknowns—by embracing mystery—the parents commit a final act of love. In keeping alive the story of their son's goodness, they retreat from reality and cross the line separating truth from faith.

In these final moments Foote, one of the most adamant realists in the history of American theater, reveals the boundaries of his realism. As he makes explicit in his lecture "The Artist as Myth-Maker," Foote believes

---

become less assured about their own motives and goals; consequently, there are fewer passages in which they explain their feelings, mistakes, and conclusions. His mature dramas have little closure; explanations, if any, are tenuous, and the endings function more as lulls than as resolutions. The human drama continues, the plays imply; only time and mystery remain.

12. Ibid., 106, 108–109.
13. Ibid., 109.

the writer should be a "truth searcher," always risking the "collision of myth and reality" he finds definitively expressed in Katherine Anne Porter's *The Old Mortality*. Even when creating fiction, Foote argues, the artist should employ myths which are not "phoney or synthetic. They must be truly rooted in a time and place to be useful . . . [and not] degenerate into stereotype." In the South this authenticity is found in "people who love to talk, who love to remember, who love to share their remembrances"; they are "the real myth makers." For Foote, even myth must be grounded in the real language, stories, and memories of living people.[14]

Yet in *The Young Man from Atlanta* the writer qualifies his realist argument, dramatizing instead the creative tension, the unresolvable dialectic, between reality and vision, knowledge and belief. On the one hand, the ending of *The Young Man from Atlanta* reiterates the need for the human spirit to be cold and hard. Lily Dale gains strength from having to face dark realities, especially the role her fantasies played in Bill's death. And Will is served by continually examining his own narcissism. Nevertheless, when Lily Dale and Will decide to remember a different Bill than the one represented by the bank receipts, they are not delusional. They are participating in the invention of their world. By choosing to look and talk no further, the parents embrace life's ineluctable mystery. After a long and painful pursuit of the truth, they are hungry for myth, in this case the myth of goodness.

Just as mystery returns Foote's characters to authentic myth—not the fatuous and sentimental fabrication of genres—it sensitizes them to the power of language. As Horton Foote says in an interview with John Di-Gaetani, "language is everything to me." Unlike many contemporary dramatists, however, he does not deconstruct language to reveal its emptiness and potential violence. Foote's work employs a phenomenology of language, in which he explores "the possibilities" of a found language, "not abstract, but made up of imagined and remembered particulars." Always interested in moving "people to reexamine and to think about each other and relationships," the writer explores the intent and effect of words in human community.[15] Once Lily Dale and Will finally become aware of

14. Horton Foote, "The Artist as Myth-Maker" (lecture at University of Texas at Arlington, November 16, 1988), 4, 5, 7, Foote Papers.

15. John DiGaetani, "Horton Foote," in *A Search for a Postmodern Theater: Interviews*

their weaknesses, the fragility of their marriage, and the mysteries of living, they are careful with what they say—to each other and about their son Bill. More accepting of themselves and things beyond their control, the couple fashion their words with a renewed respect for life itself.

The result is a play designed to make mystery integral to its dramatic effect. The various points of view, the profound uncertainty of the protagonists, and the ambiguous ending force the audience to imagine the complexity of the human situation and, finally, to reach their own conclusions. By creating dramatic lacunae which must be interpreted by active observers, Foote employs what Reynolds Price names the "method . . . of the composer": "His words are black notes on a white page—all but abstract signals to the minds of actor and audience, signs from which all participants in the effort (again all those at work on both sides of the stage or camera, including the audience) must make their own musical entity."[16] *Young Man*'s dedication to the nature of mystery—in life and art—requires viewers willing to practice both insight and judgment.

In an interview for *Post Script* which appeared in the summer of 1991, I asked Horton Foote what he feels about "life as a mystery." He answered instinctively and emphatically: "Well, I think, my God, how can you say it's not a mystery? You never know what the next day is going to bring and you just sit and wait and you do the best you can with what's there. . . . I think it is essentially naive to think that you can really control life because you can't. You may work to better certain aspects of life in a social sense . . . but there's certain 'givens' that you just have to accept, I think."[17] Because Horton Foote's drama is not highly rhetorical, his characters do not discuss such cerebral issues. But this belief in mystery informs the subtext of plays like *The Young Man from Atlanta*. Among the many conflicts his characters face, but rarely articulate, is the struggle between control and acceptance, which for some of them is resolved by embracing life as a divine mystery.

In the opening scenes *The Young Man from Atlanta* has a more theatrical look than most Horton Foote plays. Initially it is more satiric and sus-

with Contemporary Playwrights (Westport, Conn., 1991), 68; Foote, "What It Means to Be a Southern Writer," 23; Smith, "Horton Foote: A Writer's Journey," 27.

16. Price, Introduction to *Three Plays,* xi.

17. Wood, "Horton Foote: An Interview," 10.

penseful than Foote's usual Harrison chronicles. But as it drifts from such theatrical conventions, *Young Man,* like all of Foote's dedramatized work, discovers its subject by mostly disregarding plot. In its seemingly aimless and finally inconclusive story is a more compelling subject: whether a couple, portrayed as "vain and selfish" in *Lily Dale* and *Cousins,* can improve their marriage after the death of their son. They do, to a limited extent, because, as the writer says of characters in his early teleplays, they are in the process of "an acceptance of life" and "a preparation for death."[18] Such intimacy and courage in the face of death—their son's and their own—is inspired by their acceptance that finally everything, and everybody, is sacrificed to God's mysterious order.

18. Foote, Introduction to *Young Man,* xi; Foote, Preface to *Harrison, Texas,* viii.

Personal Writing and Collaborative Art

With few exceptions, Horton Foote's voices, characters, and stories come from coastal southeast Texas. The dialogue typically contains the folk-speech, understatement, and sparseness of this region. And Foote is true to its people and history, relying on the images and facts of that place. But it is misleading to reduce his writing to local color or regionalism, for Foote is a deeply personal writer whose imaginary places resonate with his private mythology. His rivers are marked by time; his prairies are parched by the loss of tradition and myth. In this dry land his orphaned characters long for the same kind of rootedness the trees possess, reaching deep into the Texas soil. They want the shelter and nourishment of homes; they thirst for emotional and spiritual water that can heal them and give them peace and contentment.

At the heart of their call for connection and intimacy is a profound need for human community. Many deny they are orphans, believing instead in financial security and control over others. Clinging to images of a God of punishment and guilt, they are unable to offer the empathy and comfort which is the foundation of community. Thus characters experience and often perpetuate racism, sexual misunderstanding and exploitation, betrayal, violence, and death. The rich exploit the poor, and poverty breeds even more confusion, powerlessness, and violence. Without a sense of place, many Foote characters lose track of their own and their culture's history; they become afraid and irresponsible. Until they develop a powerful intimate life, one based on a radical commitment to love, their social action is always compromised by their own primitive needs.

Fortunately, the male desire for distance and control in Foote's stories is tempered by the better nature of many of his women. More so than the men, these women are willing to accept things they do not understand and offer a strength born of their acceptance of life's dark realities: failure, brokenness, and death. Free to focus on what is actually within their power, they are more resilient and flexible in meeting challenges. In the process they reunite the alienated male consciousness with the mysterious natural processes. They are steadfast spiritual presences offering a benevolent witness to the lives around them. At their best, they are saints connecting the unregenerate material world with a sense of the divine.

As this view of women implies, Foote's stories call for a return to religious sensibility in an increasingly rootless land. But the experience he imagines is neither dogmatic nor evangelical. Rather, it is a deeply personal call to an intimacy which has immediate and practical application. Initially it relieves men and women of the modern obsession with absolute knowledge, power, and control. By leaving many realities with God, and by accepting the mystery of the human condition, the believer can enjoy a freer, more vital life. By offering a sense of community, religion rescues Foote's characters from the profound narcissism of our time, what he calls the "endless inward chant."[1] Most important, religious experience offers the identity and purpose that are essential to courage. And without courage his people cannot live or die in peace.

This hunger for authenticity is the basis of Foote's aesthetic of realism. It begins with materials drawn from actual human history. And it seeks to be true to dialect, speech patterns, genuine human emotion. Life, not formula, is its ideal form. But the life it imitates is often broken, chaotic. Lives are too provisional, too fragmentary; people are isolated and disconnected. And so the stories need to embrace the tradition and order offered by myth. Grounded in specific places and individual experiences, they never-

1. Foote, *Only the Heart,* 66.

110

theless seek to transcend their particularity. Foote desires to tell stories for all times and places. Therein lies his mythic realism.

At the heart of Foote's drama, what is most real in his work, is the eternal struggle between order and chaos. The life of the individual naturally moves toward disintegration; centrifugal forces are always at work. Loved ones die, and war and disease appear time and again; violence has many forms. Unfortunately, men and women often contribute to this chaos by blinding themselves to the dark realities. But, as Foote says in his preface to *Harrison, Texas,* his strongest characters battle "with their ignorances, fantasies, and insecurities to accept finally, happily or unhappily, the life around them."[2] Peace and contentment are not possible without this essential impulse toward acceptance of a transpersonal sense of order.

Foote's characters discover genuinely courageous living when they side with these forces of order. The most prevalent source of peace in Foote's plays is a loving and protective family life. As the writer has said of Elizabeth in *The Orphans' Home,* "I guess I was trying to test her and her marriage against this chaos—the chaos of poverty, of lives that have no order. And you know, the chaotic people do sense there is some order in Horace and Elizabeth, whether it's from their love or wherever."[3] When family is not sustaining, some Foote characters, like Carrie Watts, take strength from the natural world; they have faith in the process of life more than in people or institutions. Others, like Rosa Lee, believe in generation and tradition; they become deeply rooted in a particular place. And many, like Henry Vaughn, Mac Sledge, and Ludie Watts, find joy in work; it is their source of dignity and self-expression. Religion—no matter what the creed—can strengthen people by reducing their confusion. Again the author explains, "You know, a lot of difficulty comes to people in their lives, and you have to ask yourself, What gets them through it? And if you are at all honest, you have to say that you may or may not understand it, but you have to witness to the fact that their religion must sustain them a great deal."[4] Whatever the cause, Foote's people have an almost genetic need for a sense of order.

2. Foote, Preface to *Harrison, Texas,* ix.
3. David Sterritt, "Horton Foote: Filmmaking Radical with a Tender Touch," *Christian Science Monitor,* May 1986, p. 36.
4. Neff, "Going Home to the Hidden God," 30.

In every case intimacy is the foundation for the contentment desired by Foote's characters. In the face of the many forces of darkness—ignorance, self-delusion, violence, and death—they seek loving connection. Paradoxically, they find themselves and know peace only when they discover a sense of community with others. While they come home to many different places—work, the land, a religious tradition, their families—the happiest and most graceful of Foote's characters share a capacity for empathy, compassion, and comfort. Being close to whom or what they love gives them the courage to be themselves, living and dying.

Implied in this theater of intimacy is Foote's vision of God as loving, never vindictive. While he does not insist that his characters share this understanding, Foote imagines a new "spirituality" inspired by love. Like fellow playwright David Mamet, Foote asks his readers/audience to "look at the things that finally matter: we need to be loved, we need to be secure, we need to help each other, we need to work." For Foote all of these are made possible by courage; like Mamet's, his plays "try to reduce all of my perceptions of the terror around me to the proper place."[5] Horton Foote writes to discover the sources, nature, and power of courage, which is, he discovers, finally sacrificed to mystery.

But Foote's drama is not given over to such themes, even as passing thoughts. His personal vision of intimacy, identity, and courage is sublimated in his realistic presentation of historical characters and moments. The signature of this theater is a dedramatization which would make art almost photographically true to life. Talkiness, preference for privileged moments over obligatory scenes, and lack of closure are essential to his humanistic plays. Such realism rejects the artificial myths of American culture, particularly the extreme individualism of west Texas and its many cowboys. Instead it finds its characters and stories in a coastal east Texas known by its writer. Needing to remain close to the authentic experience, both in the living and in the reporting, it willingly ignores most conventions of theater and film.

But it also reflects, occasionally even embraces, secular and religious myth as a source of peace and contentment. As it crosses the threshold from personal inquiry to such mythic realism, Foote's theater becomes decidedly more attentive to its communal nature and public responsibilities.

5. Bigsby, *Modern American Drama*, 229.

When he writes for film, collaboration is obviously integral to the process. His vision is jeopardized each time the director makes naive or unsympathetic responses to the text. The politics of choosing location or casting the actors is likewise dangerous, given the musical structure and subtle subtexts of Foote's drama. Editing reshapes each performance and scene in ways unimagined in the original screenplay. Finally, distribution and exhibition are often geared for audiences addicted, under the influence of aggressive commercial interests, to the recycling of actors, roles, and situations.

Foote's work is not elitist; it recognizes that all dramatic art, not just film, relies on such risky collaboration. As the writer explains in his Fairleigh Dickinson lecture "Achieving a Sense of Place in Plays and Screenplays," the relatively confined and immediate world of the stage is as collective as moviemaking; since "plays and screenplays in production become a collaborative art, the author is often literally at the mercy and talent of the designer, the director and the actors—the playwright hopes his play or screenplay will guide everyone to the vision of his reality, to the truth of the place he is writing about, always knowing, if he is wise, that in our ever changing world and given the acknowledged even welcomed limitations of theater and film, his reality will finally have to make peace with a reality true to a collective vision."[6] According to Foote, aesthetic issues do not separate dramatic writing from poetry and fiction; both theater and literature employ words, text, and imagination. It is the "collective vision," which requires the writer to "make peace" with a product not wholly his own, that is the unique burden and opportunity of the playwright.

This shared creativity inevitably implicates the audience itself in the group performance. Believing in the ineluctable subjectivity and ambiguity of the material world, the playwright requires viewers who imagine complex human situations and create their sense of reality. Because he imagines his work as inevitably, and finally, composed from each viewer's "own musical entity," Foote invites his audiences to practice their own insight and judgment in a world imagined as both comfortingly familiar and terribly mysterious.[7] Each time active participants—whether artists or viewers—collaborate in his theater of intimacy, the playwright transforms his per-

6. MS in Foote Papers, 30.
7. Price, Introduction to *Three Plays*, xi.

sonal study of identity and courage into a public exercise of empathy and compassion.

Recognizing that his plays are inspired by the voices and stories of real people, the writer considers his work the gift of Texas storytellers, the original mythmakers. Such empathy for his subjects causes Foote to continually reexamine his assumptions, to explore the variations in each tale and theme. As his stories are staged, he also insists, whenever possible, on working with collaborators with respect for the South, including the burdens of its past and its various religious affirmations. Once performed, the plays require audiences capable of similar sensibilities. The result is a drama which at times seems anachronistic in its call for a more humane sense of community. But it is not reactionary. It is a theater designed to subvert traditional playwrighting in pursuit of a radical sympathy between art and life.

Bibliography

There are more than 140 boxes in the Horton Foote collection in the De-Golyer Library at Southern Methodist University. Included are many unpublished manuscripts, from the author's first plays for the American Actors Company to scripts for *The Gabby Hayes Show* and two novels. The following list includes the produced plays, teleplays, and screenplays and many commissioned and unproduced works, including adaptations. Fragmentary works from the DeGolyer collection are omitted, but recent plays not yet placed at SMU have been added. While the commissioned works are often much less personal than his Texas writing, these are the essential produced and unproduced works of the Foote canon. Not every production is included, but this list describes the general patterns in the presentation of Foote's works.

Plays

American Theme. Copyright 1947. "A play with music and dance." Parable-like, in five "sections": (1) "The Country," (2) "The Town," (3) "The Dream of the

City," (4) "The Old Homestead and Poor Butterfly," and (5) "The Good Samaritan and the Prodigal Son." Unproduced.

Arrival and Departure. "Curtain raiser" for HB production of *The Road to the Graveyard.* October 15–25, 1980.

Blind Date. One-act play. Produced with *The Man Who Climbed the Pecan Trees,* Loft Studio, Los Angeles, 1982. Dir. Peggy Feury. First New York production HB Playwrights Foundation, July 1985, dir. Herbert Berghof, as trilogy *Harrison, Texas,* including *The Prisoner's Song* and *Blind Date.* Also Ensemble Studio Theatre, New York, May 1986, dir. Curt Dempster.

The Brazorians. Late-1940s projected trilogy, apparently incomplete. Second play, *Emily,* published in Summer 1949 issue of *Kansas City Review.*

The Chase. First prod. and dir. José Ferrer at Playhouse Theatre, New York, April 15, 1952. Starring John Hodiak, Kim Hunter, and Kim Stanley.

A Coffin in Egypt. Originally produced 1980 at HB Playwrights Foundation, New York, as *In a Coffin in Egypt.* Dir. Horton Foote and Herbert Berghof. Starring Sandy Dennis. Also under revised title at Bay Street Theatre, Sag Harbor, N.Y., June 17–July 5, 1998. Dir. Leonard Foglia. Starring Glynis Johns.

Daisy Speed. Dance-play. Choreographed and danced by Valerie Bettis, April 1944, under title *Daisy Lee.*

The Day Emily Married, a.k.a. *Indian Fighters.* Early versions 1955–56, 1958. Revised final version, 1963. As in *Only the Heart,* a girl (Emily Davis) must leave because mother interferes. Complement to *Night Seasons.* Produced under original title at Silver Spring Stage, Silver Spring, Md., May 30–June 28, 1997. Dir. Jack Sbarbori.

Defeated. Unproduced, possibly written in late 1960s. Family adjusts to loss of election by politician father.

Dividing the Estate. Premiere March 28, 1989, at McCarter Theatre, Princeton, N.J. Dir. Jamie Brown. Also produced at Great Lakes Playhouse, Cleveland, Ohio, October 11, 1990, and Roger Stevens Theatre, Winston-Salem, North Carolina, 1991, both dir. Gerald Freedman. Early version titled *Modern Times.*

The Flowering of the Drama. Early play produced at Neighborhood Playhouse.

Getting Frankie Married—and Afterwards. Revised version July and December 1990. Unproduced.

Gone with the Wind. Musical adaptation of Margaret Mitchell novel. Performed at Drury Lane Theatre, London, 1972–73. Music and lyrics by Harold Rome. Dallas Summer Musical, June 15, 1976.

Goodbye. Also titled *Goodbye to Richmond.* Commissioned and produced at Neighborhood Playhouse, 1944, Baltimore Museum of Art and Hunter College, 1946.

The Habitation of Dragons. First produced at Pittsburgh Public Theater, September 20–October 23, 1988. Dir. Horton Foote. Starring Marco St. John, Hallie Foote, and Horton Foote Jr.

Harrison, Texas. Title given to HB Playwrights Foundation presentation of three Foote one-acts: *The One-Armed Man, The Prisoner's Song,* and *Blind Date.* HB Playwrights Foundation, New York, July 9–22, 1985.

Homecoming. Produced in Washington, D.C., 1944, and later off-Broadway.

In My Beginning. Early unproduced play described as "A Miracle Play with Music and Dance" set in present and focusing on view of a loving, rather than a punishing, God.

John Turner Davis. Originally teleplay for *Philco Television Playhouse,* 1953. Produced off-Broadway at Sheridan Square Playhouse, 1956.

Land of the Astronauts. One-act play. First production Ensemble Studio Theatre, New York, May 1988. Dir. Curt Dempster.

Laura Dennis. Produced by Signature Theatre Company, New York, March 10–April 9, 1995. Dir. James Houghton. Starring Missy Yager and Hallie Foote.

The Lonely. Play with dance for Neighborhood Playhouse, co-dir. by Foote and Martha Graham, 1944.

The Man Who Climbed the Pecan Trees. First production Loft Studio, Los Angeles, 1982, with *Blind Date.* Dir. William Traylor. Starring Peggy Feury and Albert Horton Foote. First New York production Ensemble Studio Theatre, July 1988, dir. Curt Dempster.

Marcus Strachen. Unproduced play for American Actors Company in mid-1940s. Deals with racism and upward mobility in late 1800s.

The Midnight Caller. Originally teleplay for *Philco Television Playhouse,* 1953. Produced off-Broadway at Sheridan Square Playhouse, 1956. Also at Neighborhood Playhouse, starring Robert Duvall.

Miss Lou. Produced at Neighborhood Playhouse, dir. Sanford Meisner, 1943.

Night Seasons. Produced at HB Playwrights Foundation, 1978. Premiered by American Stage Company, Teaneck, N.J., February 26, 1993. Dir. Horton Foote. Starring Hallie Foote and Jean Stapleton. In Signature Theatre Series, November 4–December 4, 1994, with same director and stars.

The Old Friends. Produced at HB Playwrights Foundation, July 27–August 7, 1982.

The One-Armed Man. One-act play. Produced July 1985, HB Playwrights Foundation, New York, as part of *Harrison, Texas* trilogy, with *The Prisoner's Song* and *Blind Date.* Dir. Herbert Berghof.

Only the Heart. Originally titled *Mamie Borden,* produced by American Actors Company, Provincetown Playhouse, New York, 1942–44. Dir. Mary Hunter. Starring Mildred Dunnock and June Walker. Also on Broadway, 1944.

The Orphans' Home (nine-play cycle): Early version called *The Sea of Glass:* (1) *Roots in a Parched Ground;* (2) *Convicts;* (3) *Lily Dale,* reading at Ensemble Studio Theatre, 1977, produced Samuel Beckett Theatre, New York, November 1986. Starring Molly Ringwald; (4) *The Widow Claire,* prod. Circle in the Square Theatre, New York, 1986, dir. Michael Lindsay-Hogg. Starring Matthew Broderick and Hallie Foote; (5) *Courtship,* prod. HB Playwrights Foundation, New York, July 5–16, 1978, dir. Horton Foote. Also Actors Theatre, Louisville, Ky., 1984, and Dallas (Tex.) Contemporary American Theatre; (6) *Valentine's Day,* prod. HB Playwrights Foundation, New York, 1980. Also Dallas (Tex.) Contemporary American Theatre, February 27–April 7, 1985; (7) *1918,* prod. HB Playwrights Foundation, dir. Horton Foote. Also A.C.T. Theatre, San Francisco, 1991; (8) *Cousins,* prod. Loft Theatre, Los Angeles, 1983; (9) *The Death of Papa,* premiered by Playmakers Repertory Company, Chapel Hill, N.C., February 8, 1997, dir. Michael Wilson. Starring Nicholas Shaw, Hallie Foote, Matthew Broderick, Ellen Burstyn, Ray Virta, and Polly Holliday.

Out of My House. Four one-act plays produced by American Actors Company at Provincetown Playhouse, New York: *Night after Night, Celebration, The Girls, Behold a Cry.* Also considered four-part single play, 1942. *Celebration* also produced at ANTA Theatre, New York, 1950.

People in the Show. Produced in Washington, D.C., in late 1940s. Set at New York World's Fair, May 1940.

Pilgrims. Dance-play for Agnes de Mille. In progress 1964–65, 1968–74. Unproduced.

The Prisoner's Song. One-act play. Produced July 1985, HB Playwrights Foundation, New York. Dir. by Herbert Berghof. Produced with *The One-Armed Man* and *Blind Date* as trilogy titled *Harrison, Texas.*

The Return. Prod. King-Smith Productions, Washington, D.C., in late 1940s. Early version of *In a Coffin in Egypt.*

The Road to the Graveyard. First draft early 1950. Produced at HB Playwrights Foundation, New York, 1982, and Ensemble Studio Theatre, New York, May 1985. Dir. Curt Dempster.

The Roads to Home (trilogy of one-act plays): *A Nightingale, The Dearest of Friends,* and *Spring Dance.* First produced Manhattan Punch Line Theatre, New York, March 25, 1982. Dir. Calvin Skaggs. Starring Carol Fox, Rochelle Oliver, and Hallie Foote. Also at Lambs Theatre, New York, September 1992, for which Hallie Foote won 1993 Obie Award.

Roundabout. Ballet with Jerome Robbins, 1953. Produced in Broadway musical *Two for the Show.*

Selina Peake. Unproduced commissioned play for Robert Friar. Adaptation of Edna Ferber's *So Big.* To star Shirley Booth.

Summer of the Hot Five. Unproduced play based on brothers (George and Leonard Payne) in *Habitation of Dragons.* Leonard loses family money but George forgives him and goes back to playing in band.

Talking Pictures. First produced at Asolo Theater, Sarasota, Fla., 1990. Dir. John Ulmer. Also Stages Theatre, Houston, 1991, and first play in Signature Theatre Series, September 23–October 23, 1994, dir. Carol Goodheart.

Texas Town. First full-length play. Prod. American Actors Company, dir. Mary Hunter, 1941.

Themes and Variations. Prod. King-Smith Workshop, Washington, D.C., in late 1940s.

Tomorrow. Stage version of teleplay. Presented by the HB Playwrights Foundation, April–May 1968. Dir. Herbert Berghof. Starring Robert Duvall and Olga Bellin.

The Traveling Lady. Prod. Playwrights' Company, at the Playhouse, New York, October 27, 1954. Dir. Vincent J. Donehue. Starring Kim Stanley and Lonny Chapman. Later produced at Alley Theatre, Houston, 1986. Also produced as teleplay with same title and as film titled *Baby, the Rain Must Fall.*

The Trip to Bountiful. Produced by the Theatre Guild and Fred Coe at Henry Miller's Theatre, New York, November 3, 1953. Dir. Vincent J. Donehue and starring Lillian Gish, Jo Van Fleet, and Eva Marie Saint. Also teleplay in March 1953. Also produced at Greenwich Mews Theatre, New York, 1962; A.D. Players, Houston, and Zachary Scott Theatre, Austin, Tex., both in 1990; Actors Theatre, Louisville, Ky., and New Harmony (Ind.) Theatre, 1991; Theatre Festival, Perth, Australia, 1992; TheatreFest, Upper Montclair, N.J., 1993; Phoenix Theatre Company, Purchase, N.Y., 1993.

Two's Company. Theatre revue starring Bette Davis, 1953.

Vernon Early. Premiere by Alabama Shakespeare Festival, Montgomery, May 26–July 26, 1998. Dir. Charles Towers. Starring Jill Tanner and Philip Pleasants.

Wharton Dance. First one-act play. Written and produced by American Actors Company, 1939–40.

The Young Man from Atlanta. Prod. Signature Theatre Company, New York, January 27–February 26, 1995. Awarded Pulitzer Prize for drama. Also produced at Alley Theatre, Houston, 1996, dir. Peter Masterson, and starring Ralph Waite and Carlin Glynn; Goodman Theatre, Chicago, January 1997, dir. Robert Falls, and starring Shirley Knight and Rip Torn, restaged at Longacre Theatre, New York, with same dir. and stars, March 1997. Nominated for Tony Award.

Teleplays

Alone. Original teleplay for Showtime Television, 1997, starring Hume Cronyn, James Earl Jones, and Piper Laurie. Man in seventies finds courage to deal with loss of wife, asking his children to pursue their own lives while he finds comfort in religion he shares with black friends.

Barn Burning. Adaptation of William Faulkner story for *American Short Story* series on PBS, March 17, 1980. Dir. Peter Werner. Starring Tommy Lee Jones and Diane Kagan.

A Christmas Story. Two-hour teleplay based on Norman Rockwell characters for Concepts Unlimited. Completed February 1979. Unproduced.

The Dancers. On *Philco Television Playhouse,* NBC, March 7, 1954. Prod. Fred Coe, dir. Vincent J. Donehue. Starring Joanne Woodward and James Broderick.

The Death of the Old Man. On *First Person Playhouse,* NBC, July 17, 1953. Prod. Fred Coe, dir. Arthur Penn. Starring Mildred Natwick and William Hanson.

Displaced Person. Adaptation of Flannery O'Connor short story for PBS *American Short Story* series. Dir. Glenn Jordan. Starring Irene Worth and John Houseman. Broadcast April 14, 1980.

Drug Store, Sunday Noon. Commissioned adaptation of Robert Hutchinson short story. *Omnibus,* ABC, December 16, 1956. Dir. Andrew McCullough. Starring Helen Hayes.

The Edna Harris Story. Commissioned by Alan Landsburg Productions for network television. Unproduced.

The Expectant Relations. On *Philco Television Playhouse,* NBC, June 21, 1953. Prod. Fred Coe, dir. Vincent J. Donehue.

Flight. On *Playwrights '56,* NBC, February 28, 1956. Prod. Fred Coe, dir. Vincent J. Donehue. Starring Kim Stanley.

The Gambling Heart. On *Du Pont Show of the Week,* NBC, February 23, 1964. Prod. David Susskind and Daniel Melnick, dir. Paul Bogart. Starring Tom Bosley and Estelle Parsons.

The Grass Harp. Commissioned adaptation of Truman Capote novel for KCET-TV, 1982. Unproduced.

The Habitation of Dragons. For *Writer's Cinema,* Amblin-Steven Spielberg Production, TNT, Spring 1992. Teleplay from Foote play with same title. Dir. Michael Lindsay-Hogg and starring Brad Davis, Jean Stapleton, Frederic Forrest, Pat Hingle, Hallie Foote, and Horton Foote Jr.

John Turner Davis. On *Goodyear Television Playhouse,* NBC, November 5, 1953. Prod. Fred Coe, dir. Arthur Penn.

Keeping On. Presented by PBS *American Playhouse,* 1983. Prod. and dir. Barbara Kopple.

Kip and the Colonel. Pilot for projected series about child as member of circus company. Prod. Martin Stone.

Ludie Brooks. On *Lamp unto My Feet,* CBS, February 4, 1951. Prod. Pamela Ilott, dir. Herbert Kenwith.

Lyndon. Unproduced teleplay on early life of Lyndon Johnson. Commissioned by Edgar Lansbury. Early versions 1973–74. Revised 1976. Final version April 18, 1977. Early title *Sam Johnson and Son.*

A Member of the Family. On *Studio One,* CBS, March 25, 1957. Prod. Herbert Brodkin, dir. Norman Felton. Starring Hume Cronyn and James Broderick.

The Midnight Caller. On *Philco Television Playhouse,* NBC, December 13, 1953. Prod. Fred Coe, dir. Vincent J. Donehue.

The Night of the Storm. On *Du Pont Show of the Month,* March 21, 1961. Prod. David Susskind, dir. Daniel Petrie. Starring Julie Harris, E. G. Marshall, Mildred Dunnock, Mark Connelly, Fritz Weaver, and Jo Van Fleet. Orig. title *A Golden String;* also called *Roots in a Parched Ground.*

The Oil Well. On *Goodyear Theatre,* NBC, May 17, 1953. Prod. Fred Coe, dir. Vincent J. Donehue. Starring Dorothy Gish and E. G. Marshall.

The Old Beginning. On *Goodyear Theatre,* NBC, November 23, 1952. Dir. Vincent J. Donehue. Early version called *Nature of the Beast.*

Old Man. Adaptation of William Faulkner story. *Playhouse 90,* CBS, November 20, 1958. Prod. Fred Coe, dir. John Frankenheimer. Starring Geraldine Page and Sterling Hayden. Revised version on *Hallmark Playhouse,* February 9, 1997. Prod. Brent Shields, dir. John Kent Harrison. Starring Jeanne Tripplehorn and Arliss Howard. Emmy Award.

Only the Heart. On *Kraft Television Theatre,* NBC, January 21, 1948.

The Quaker Oats Show. Forty scripts for Gabby Hayes weekly television show also called *The Gabby Hayes Show.* October 15, 1950–December 23, 1951.

The Roads to Home. On *U.S. Steel Hour,* ABC, April 26, 1955. Early teleplay different from later trilogy of one-acts with same title.

The Rocking Chair. NBC, May 24, 1953, starring Mildred Natwick and Ian Keith (aired on series *The Doctor*).

The Shadow of Willie Greer. On *Philco Television Playhouse,* NBC, May 30, 1954. Prod. Fred Coe, dir. Vincent Donehue. Starring Dorothy Gish, Pat Hingle, and Wright King. Originally titled *The Shadow of Willie Mayes.*

The Shape of the River. On *Playhouse 90,* CBS, May 2, 1960. Prod. Fred Coe. Starring Franchot Tone and Leif Erickson. Early versions called *Mark Twain.*

The Story of a Marriage. PBS *American Playhouse* five-part series based on films *Courtship, On Valentine's Day,* and *1918.* April 1987.

The Tears of My Sister. On *First Person Playhouse,* NBC, August 14, 1953. Prod. Fred Coe, dir. Arthur Penn. Starring Kim Stanley (in voice-over) and Lenka Peterson.

Tomorrow. On *Playhouse 90,* CBS, March 7, 1960. Prod. Herbert Brodkin, dir. Robert Mulligan. Based on William Faulkner story. Starring Kim Stanley,

Richard Boone, Charles Bickford, Chill Wills, and Beulah Bondi. Also play and film under same title.

The Travelers. On *Goodyear Theatre,* NBC, April 27, 1952. Prod. Fred Coe, dir. Delbert Mann. Also telecast March 7, 1954, on *Philco Television Playhouse.* Prod. Fred Coe, dir. Vincent Donehue.

The Traveling Lady. On *Studio One,* CBS, April 22, 1957. Prod. Herbert Brodkin, dir. Robert Mulligan. Starring Kim Stanley, Steven Hill, Robert Loggia, Wendy Hiller, and Mildred Dunnock. Kim Stanley won Sylvania Award for her performance. Also stage play and filmed as *Baby, the Rain Must Fall.*

The Trip to Bountiful. On *Goodyear Theatre,* NBC, March 1, 1953. Prod. Fred Coe, dir. Vincent Donehue. Starring Lillian Gish and Eva Marie Saint.

A Young Lady of Property. On *Philco Television Playhouse,* NBC, April 5, 1953. Prod. Fred Coe, dir. Vincent J. Donehue. Starring Kim Stanley and Joanne Woodward.

Screenplays

April Morning. Unproduced, adaptation of Revolutionary War novel by Howard Fast, commissioned by Samuel Goldwyn Jr., 1970–72.

Baby, the Rain Must Fall. Adaptation of Foote play *The Traveling Lady.* Prod. Alan J. Pakula, dir. Robert Mulligan. Starring Steve McQueen and Lee Remick. Columbia Pictures, 1965.

Bessie. Based on life of blues singer Bessie Smith. Early version spring 1974 for Portable Productions. Revised 1989 for WVF Productions (Walter Foote). Unproduced.

Bill W. Unproduced, commissioned, based on the life of founder of Alcoholics Anonymous, 1975–76.

The Chase. Late revisions to 1965 screenplay by Lillian Hellman from Foote play of same title. Prod. Sam Spiegel, dir. Arthur Penn. Starring Marlon Brando, Robert Redford, Jane Fonda, Angie Dickinson, and Robert Duvall. Horizon Pictures, 1966.

Children of Pride. Commissioned work for Universal, November 1975. Plantation family in remote Georgia, 1859–68. Deals with stresses on both white and black families in Civil War era. Unproduced.

Comrades. Screenplay, 1982. Earlier version called *Spanish Journey.* About volunteers for Spanish Civil War. Unproduced.

Convicts. Based on *The Orphans' Home* play of same title. Dir. Peter Masterson. Starring Robert Duvall, James Earl Jones, and Lukas Haas. Prod. Jonathan Krane and Sterling VanWagenen. MCEG-Sterling, 1990.

Courtship. From *The Orphans' Home* play of same title. Prod. Lillian V. Foote and

Marcus Viscidi, dir. Howard Cummings. Starring Hallie Foote, Amanda Plummer, Rochelle Oliver, Michael Higgins, and William Converse-Roberts. Indian Falls, 1986.

Dragon Fly. Unproduced adaptation of Will Campbell novel *Brother to a Dragonfly.* Commissioned by Tom Moore for Tomorrow Entertainment. July 1978.

Emma. Adaptation of Flaubert's *Madame Bovary* for Roland Joffe, drafted 1989. Unproduced.

Fool's Parade. Commissioned adaptation of David Grubb novel for MGM, 1969. Unproduced.

Go East, Young Man. Commissioned for Palomar Pictures. Based on autobiography of Justice William O. Douglas. In progress 1974, completed May 29, 1975. Unproduced.

The Governor's Lady. Unproduced commissioned screenplay for Tri-Star Pictures. Early drafts and revisions 1984–85. About adjustments of new wife to political realities of job.

Home Movies. Dialogue for 1971 script about divorced couple who live across from each other. New wife watches home movies of previous marriage.

Hurry Sundown. Early versions commissioned by Otto Preminger. 1965–67. Foote's script not used in film, though his name is retained. Released in 1967 by Paramount.

Jenny. In progress July 1977. Also called *The Seduction of Jenny* and *Many Mansions.* Based on Civil War letters. About sexual and racial violence in dying plantation society.

Lily Dale. Screenplay for play in *Orphans' Home* with same title. Prod. Soisson Murphy and Walter Foote, dir. Charles Martin Smith. Not completed. Later prod. and released in June 1996 for Showtime and dir. Peter Masterson. Starring Mary Stuart Masterson, Sam Shepard, Stockard Channing, Tim Guinee, and Jean Stapleton.

Little House on the Prairie. Commissioned by Universal Pictures, based on Laura Ingalls Wilder original story, not television series. In progress 1996–97.

Lone Heart Mountain. Commissioned by Jerome Hellman Productions, Inc. About Japanese internment camps during World War II. Completed November 1984, to be dir. Michael Apted. Unproduced.

The Man of the House. Orig. screenplay about black family in small southern town, for Eddie Murphy Productions. Paramount, 1994. Unproduced.

Of Mice and Men. Adaptation of Steinbeck novel. Dir. Gary Sinise. Starring John Malkovich and Gary Sinise. Released 1992 by MGM.

1918. Screenplay based on play from *Orphans' Home* cycle with same title. Prod. Lewis Allen, Peter Newman, and Lillian Foote, dir. Ken Harrison. Starring

Matthew Broderick, William Converse-Roberts, and Hallie Foote. Guadalupe Entertainment and Cinecom, 1985.

On Valentine's Day. Adaptation of Foote play *Valentine's Day* from *Orphans' Home* cycle. Prod. Lillian V. Foote and Calvin Skaggs, dir. Ken Harrison. Starring William Converse-Roberts, Matthew Broderick, and Hallie Foote. 1986.

Ordeal by Hunger. Revised 1962. Completed for Stuart Millar, 1966. Unproduced. Families on wagon train west to California deal with class consciousness and cannibalism.

Pastor's Son. Original screenplay for production by Wind Dancer Films, 1993. Adjustments made within family of Lutheran minister. Unproduced.

Roots in the Parched Ground. Unproduced screenplay, first draft July 1, 1987, revised 1988–89, from Foote play in the *Orphans' Home* cycle.

Savannah. Unproduced, commissioned for Lorimar Productions, 1977.

Spring Moon. Adaptation of novel by Bette Bao Lord. Commissioned by Alan Pakula and Jake Ebertz. Early versions late 1985, drafts 1986–87. Unproduced.

The Stalking Moon. First draft completed September 14, 1967. Foote's version not used; final script completed in December 1967 by Alvin Sargent. Dir. Robert Mulligan. Released 1968 by National General.

Storm Fear. Adaptation of Clinton Seeley novel. Prod. and dir. Cornel Wilde for Theodora Productions. Released by United Artists, 1956.

Tender Mercies. Original screenplay. Dir. Bruce Beresford. Starring Robert Duvall, Tess Harper, Betty Buckley, Ellen Barkin, Wilford Brimley. Academy Award winner for best original screenplay, 1983–84. Writers Guild Award for original screenplay. Christopher Award for best picture. Antron Media-EMI, 1982. Released by Universal, 1982. American entry in Cannes Film Festival, 1983. Robert Duvall also won best actor Oscar for film.

This Property Is Condemned. Unproduced 1962 adaptation of Tennessee Williams play.

Through Another Window. Also called *Rapid Change.* Commissioned work about labor organization against J. P. Stevens textile company. In progress 1980. Unproduced.

To Kill a Mockingbird. Adaptation of Harper Lee novel. Prod. Alan J. Pakula, dir. Robert Mulligan. Starring Gregory Peck. Universal, 1963. Academy Award for best screenplay based on material from another medium. Writer's Guild of America Award for best American drama. American entry in 1963 Cannes Film Festival. Gregory Peck won Academy Award for best actor.

Tomorrow. Adaptation of William Faulkner story. Prod. Paul Roebling and Gilbert Pearlman, dir. Joseph Anthony. Starring Robert Duvall and Olga Bellin. Filmgroup, 1972.

The Trip to Bountiful. Based on Foote play of same title. Prod. Sterling VanWagenen, dir. Peter Masterson. Starring Geraldine Page, John Heard, Carlin
Glynn, Richard Bradford, and Rebecca DeMornay. Island Pictures, 1985. Film
for which Geraldine Page won her only Academy Award. Nominated for best
adaptation by Academy and Writers Guild.

The Widow Claire. Unproduced screenplay from *Orphan's Home* play of same title.
Revised December 20, 1988. Completed August 1, 1990.

Other Works

"Achieving a Sense of Place in Plays and Screenplays." Lecture at Fairleigh Dickinson College, March 30, 1987.

"The Artist as Myth-Maker." Lecture at University of Texas at Arlington, November 16, 1988.

Days of Violence. Unpublished novel. Drafts in 1964, 1969, 1972.

Lectures at Louisiana State University, Baton Rouge: "Listening and Imagining,"
April 19, 1989; "Pasadena and Beyond," April 20, 1989; "Learning to Write,"
April 21, 1989.

"The Little Box." Draft of short essay on opportunities and limitations of working
in early television.

"What It Means to Be a Southern Writer." Lecture for SECA (Southern Educational Communication Authority), n.p., n.d.

PUBLISHED WORKS BY HORTON FOOTE

Blind Date. New York: Dramatists Play Service, 1986.

The Chase. New York: Dramatists Play Service, 1952.

The Chase [novel]. New York: Rinehart, 1956.

Courtship. New York: Dramatists Play Service, 1984.

*"Courtship," "Valentine's Day," "1918": Three Plays from "The Orphans' Home"
Cycle.* Introduction by Reynolds Price. New York: Grove Press, 1987.

Cousins. New York: Dramatists Play Service, 1989.

"Cousins" and "The Death of Papa": Two Plays from The Orphans' Home Cycle. Introduction by Samuel G. Freedman. New York: Grove Press, 1989.

The Death of Papa. New York: Dramatists Play Service, 1989.

Emily [play for projected trilogy *The Brazorians*], *Kansas City Review,* XV (Summer
1949), 263–66.

Farewell: A Memoir of a Texas Childhood. New York: Scribner, 1999.

"Father's Store." *Countryside,* II (Summer 1991), 4.

Bibliography

"Flight." *Television Plays for Writers.* Edited by Abraham Burack. Boston: The Writer, 1957.

Four Plays from "The Orphans' Home" Cycle. Introduction by Horton Foote. New York: Grove Press, 1988 [*Roots in a Parched Ground, Convicts, Lily Dale, The Widow Claire*].

Habitation of Dragons. New York: Dramatists Play Service, 1993.

Harrison, Texas: Eight Television Plays. Preface by Horton Foote. New York: Harcourt Brace, 1956 [*A Young Lady of Property, John Turner Davis, The Tears of My Sister, The Death of the Old Man, Expectant Relations, The Midnight Caller, The Dancers, The Trip to Bountiful*].

Horton Foote: Collected Plays. Introduction by Robert Ellermann. Lyme, N.H.: Smith and Kraus, 1996 [*The Trip to Bountiful, The Chase, The Traveling Lady, The Roads to Home*].

Horton Foote: Four New Plays. Introduction by Jerry Tallmer. Newbury, Vt.: Smith and Kraus, 1993 [*The Habitation of Dragons, Night Seasons, Dividing the Estate, Talking Pictures*].

Horton Foote: "Getting Frankie Married—And Afterwards" and Other Plays. Introduction by James Houghton. Lyme, N.H.: Smith and Kraus, 1998 [*The Day Emily Married, Tomorrow, A Coffin in Egypt, Laura Dennis, Vernon Early, Getting Frankie Married—And Afterwards*].

Horton Foote: Three Plays. New York: Harcourt Brace and World, 1962 [*Old Man, Tomorrow, Roots in a Parched Ground*].

Horton Foote's Three Trips to Bountiful. Edited by Barbara Moore and David G. Yellin. Dallas: Southern Methodist University Press, 1993 [play, teleplay, and screenplay].

Laura Dennis. New York: Dramatists Play Service, 1996.

Lily Dale. New York: Dramatists Play Service, 1987.

"The Long, Long Trek." *Dance Observer,* XI (October 1944), 98–99. [Foote asks artists in dance to avoid temptations of "finance capitalism" and stay true to talent and vision.]

The Man Who Climbed Pecan Trees. New York: Dramatists Play Service, 1989.

The Midnight Caller. New York: Dramatists Play Service, 1959.

Night Seasons. New York: Dramatists Play Service, 1996.

1918. New York: Dramatists Play Service, 1987.

"Old Man" and "Tomorrow." New York: Dramatists Play Service, 1963.

"On First Dramatizing Faulkner." In *Faulkner, Modernism, and Film: Faulkner and Yoknapatawpha, 1978,* edited by Evans Harrington and Ann J. Abadie. Jackson: University Press of Mississippi, 1979.

"On Writing and Risks." In *An Ear to the Ground: Presenting Writers from Two Coasts,* edited by Katie Davis and Scott C. Davis. Seattle: Cune, 1997.

Only the Heart. New York: Dramatists Play Service, 1944.

The Road to the Graveyard. New York: Dramatists Play Service, 1988.

The Roads to Home. New York: Dramatists Play Service, 1982.

Roots in a Parched Ground. New York: Dramatists Play Service, 1962.

"Roots in a Parched Ground," "Convicts," "Lily Dale," "The Widow Claire": The First Four Plays of "The Orphans' Home" Cycle. Introduction by Horton Foote. New York: Grove Press, 1988.

Selected One-Act Plays of Horton Foote. Edited by Gerald C. Wood. Dallas: Southern Methodist University Press, 1989 [*The Old Beginning, A Young Lady of Property, The Oil Well, The Death of the Old Man, The Tears of My Sister, John Turner Davis, The Midnight Caller, The Dancers, The Man Who Climbed Pecan Trees, The Roads to Home (A Nightingale, The Dearest of Friends,* and *Spring Dance), Blind Date, The Prisoner's Song, The One-Armed Man, The Road to the Graveyard, The Land of the Astronauts*].

"Sometimes the One-act Play Says It All." *New York Times,* May 4, 1986, sec. 2, p. 7.

Talking Pictures. New York: Dramatists Play Service, 1996.

"The Tears of My Sister," "The Prisoner's Song," "The One-Armed Man," and "The Land of the Astronauts." New York: Dramatists Play Service, 1993.

"Texas Towns Lost and Found." *From Uncertain to Blue.* With photographs by Keith Carter. Austin: Texas Monthly Press, 1988.

To Kill a Mockingbird [screenplay]. New York: Harcourt Brace and World, 1964.

Three Screenplays: "To Kill a Mockingbird," "Tender Mercies," and "The Trip to Bountiful." Foreword by Horton Foote. New York: Grove Press, 1989.

Tomorrow [play]. New York: Dramatists Play Service, 1963.

"Tomorrow: The Genesis of a Screenplay." In *Faulkner, Modernism and Film: Faulkner and Yoknapatawpha,* edited by Evans Harrington and Ann J. Abadie. Jackson: University Press of Mississippi, 1979.

Tomorrow and Tomorrow and Tomorrow. Edited by David G. Yellin and Marie Connors. Jackson: University Press of Mississippi, 1985 [play, teleplay, and screenplay].

The Traveling Lady. New York: Dramatists Play Service, 1955.

"The Trip from Wharton." In *Backstory 3: Interviews with Screenwriters of the 1960s.* Berkeley: University of California Press, 1997.

The Trip to Bountiful. New York: Dramatists Play Service, 1954.

"The Trip to Paradise." *Texas Monthly,* December 1987, pp. 140–49, 182–83.

Valentine's Day. New York: Dramatists Play Service, 1987.

The Widow Claire. New York: Dramatists Play Service, 1987.

"Writing for Film." In *Film and Literature: A Comparative Approach to Adaptation,* edited by Wendell Aycock and Michael Schoenecke. Lubbock: Texas Tech University Press, 1988.

A Young Lady of Property [six short plays]. New York: Dramatists Play Service, 1983 [*A Young Lady of Property, The Dancers, The Oil Well, The Old Beginning, Death of the Old Man,* and *John Turner Davis*].

The Young Man from Atlanta. New York: Dramatists Play Service, 1995.

The Young Man from Atlanta. Introduction by Horton Foote. New York: Dutton, 1995.

WORKS ABOUT HORTON FOOTE

The bibliography of writing about Horton Foote, as for any writer in popular arts like television and film, is nearly inexhaustible. There are, for example, reviews in newspapers and magazines wherever his plays have been staged or his films shown. Consequently, this list represents primarily academic writing about the author, as well as other material, including journalistic work, that was especially useful for this study. But personal interviews and videotapes are omitted in the interest of space, as are anthologies which include at least one Foote play.

Barbera, Jack. "Tomorrow and Tomorrow and *Tomorrow.*" In *The South and Film,* edited by Warren French. Jackson, Miss., 1981. Originally published in *Southern Quarterly,* XIX (Spring–Summer 1981), 183–97.

Barr, Terry. "Horton Foote's TV Women: The Richest Part of a Golden Age." In *Horton Foote: A Casebook,* edited by Gerald C. Wood. New York, 1997, pp. 35–47.

———. "The Ordinary World of Horton Foote." Ph.D. dissertation, University of Tennessee, 1987.

Benson, Sheila. "Horton Foote." Interview. *Modern Maturity,* November–December 1996, pp. 52–57.

Blake, Richard A. "Texas Agape." *America,* April 23, 1983, p. 322.

Borchard, Fredrika D. "Horton from Wharton." *Houston Chronicle Rotogravure Magazine,* October 4, 1953, pp. 6–7.

Brian, Crystal. "The Roads to Home: Material, Method, and Meditation in Horton Foote's *The Orphans' Home.*" Ph.D. dissertation, University of California at Los Angeles, 1993.

———. " 'To Be Quiet and Listen': *The Orphans' Home Cycle* and the Music of Charles Ives." In *Horton Foote: A Casebook,* edited by Gerald C. Wood. New York, 1997, pp. 89–108.

Briley, Rebecca. "Southern Accents: Horton Foote's Adaptations of William

Faulkner, Harper Lee, and Flannery O'Connor." In *Horton Foote: A Casebook,* edited by Gerald C. Wood. New York, 1997, pp. 49–65.

———. "You Can Go Home Again: The Focus on Family in the Works of Horton Foote." Ph.D. dissertation, University of Kentucky, 1990.

———. *You Can Go Home Again: The Focus on Family in the Works of Horton Foote.* New York, 1993.

Broughton, Irv. "Horton Foote." In *The Writer's Mind: Interviews with American Writers,* edited by Irv Broughton. Vol. II. Fayetteville, Ark., 1990.

Burkhart, Marian. "Horton Foote's Many Roads Home: An American Playwright and His Characters." *Commonweal,* February 26, 1988, pp. 110–15.

Calio, Jim, and David Hutchings. "Drawing on His Clan's Past, Writer Horton Foote Unearths an Oscar-winning Bounty." *People,* June 9, 1986, pp. 71, 73–74.

Canby, Vincent. "Film: 'Valentine's Day' from Horton Foote." *New York Times,* April 11, 1986, sec. C, p. 8.

———. "For Horton Foote the Pictures Speak Volumes." *New York Times,* October 2, 1994, sec. H, pp. 5, 14.

Castleberry, Marion. "Remembering Wharton, Texas." In *Horton Foote: A Casebook,* edited by Gerald C. Wood. New York, 1997, pp. 13–33.

———. "Voices from Home: Familial Bonds in the Works of Horton Foote." Ph.D. dissertation, Louisiana State University, 1993.

Chappell, Fred. "Understand Me Completely." *Chronicles,* XIII (November 1989), 35–37.

Charlotte, Susan. "Carlin Glynn and Peter Masterson [on *Trip to Bountiful*]." In *Creativity.* Troy, Mich., 1993, pp. 106–24.

"*Christianity Today* Talks to Horton Foote." *Christianity Today,* April 4, 1986, p. 30.

Daily, Bob. "The Heart and Soul of Horton Foote." *Ultra,* VII (November 1987), 54–57, 88.

Darnton, Nina. "Horton Foote Celebrates a Bygone America in *1918.*" *New York Times,* April 21, 1985, sec. 2, pp. 17, 22.

Davis, Ronald L. "Roots in Parched Ground: An Interview with Horton Foote." *Southwest Review,* LXXIII (Summer 1988), 298–318.

Desser, David. "Transcendental Style in *Tender Mercies.*" *Religious Communication Today,* September 1985, pp. 21–27.

DiGaetani, John L. "Horton Foote." In *A Search for a Postmodern Theater: Interviews with Contemporary Playwrights.* Westport, Conn., 1991.

Edgerton, Gary. "A Visit to the Imaginary Landscape of Harrison, Texas: Sketching the Film Career of Horton Foote." *Literature/Film Quarterly,* XVII (1989), 2–12.

Flippo, Chet. "A Foote Family Affair." *New York Times,* April 5, 1987, sec. H, pp. 31–36.

Flynn, Robert, and Susan Russell. "Horton Foote." Interview. *Southern Partisan,* XII (1992), 30–34.

———. "Horton Foote." Interview. In *When I Was Just Your Age.* Denton, Tex., 1992.

"Horton Foote." Interview. *American Film,* XII (October 1986), 13–14, 16.

Forsberg, Myra. "Hallie Foote Relives Her Family's Past." *New York Times,* April 13, 1986, sec. 2, pp. 21–22.

Freedman, Samuel G. "From the Heart of Texas." *New York Times Magazine,* February 9, 1986, pp. 30–31, 50, 61–63, 73.

———. Introduction to *"Cousins" and "The Death of Papa": Two Plays from "The Orphans' Home" Cycle.* New York, 1989.

Gallagher, Michael. "Horton Foote." Interview. *Cleveland Edition,* October 4, 1990, p. 12.

Gangelhoff, Bonnie. "Horton Foote: Hometown Hero." *Magazine of the Houston Post,* November 23, 1986, pp. 6–9, 17.

Gerard, Jeremy. "Mamet, Foote and Words on Film." *New York Times,* October 8, 1986, sec. C, p. 19.

Grenader, Nonya, and Terrence Doody. "A Conversation with Horton Foote." In *Texas Places,* edited by Nonya Grenader and Bruce C. Webb. Houston, 1997.

Hachem, Samir. "Foote-Work." *Horizon,* XXIX (April 1986), 39–41.

"Horton and Hallie Foote Collaborate on *Night Seasons* at Signature Theatre." *Back Stage,* November 25, 1994, p. 13.

Hunter, Mary. Foreword to *Only the Heart,* by Horton Foote. New York, 1944.

Iturralde, Fernando A. "The Role of Horace in Horton Foote's *1918:* A Production Thesis in Acting." M.F.A. thesis, Louisiana State University, 1990.

Jayroe, Tashia. "Footeprints: A Comparison of the Teleplay and Stage Play Versions of *The Trip to Bountiful.*" M.S. thesis, East Texas State University, 1991.

Jewett, Robert. "The Mysterious God of *Tender Mercies.*" In *Saint Paul at the Movies.* Louisville, Ky., 1993.

Kart, Larry. "Horton Foote's *On Valentine's Day* a Family Project, Conception to Finish." *Chicago Tribune,* April 27, 1986, sec. 13, pp. 22–23.

King, Kimball. "Performing *The Death of Papa:* A Review." In *Horton Foote: A Casebook,* edited by Gerald C. Wood. New York, 1997, pp. 131–35.

Lee, Harper. "A Word." Introduction to *To Kill a Mockingbird* (screenplay), by Horton Foote. New York, 1964.

Leslie, Candace. "Horton Foote, Texas Bard." *Texas Highways,* February 1988, pp. 20–23.

Bibliography

Leydon, Joe. "Best Foote Forward: Playwright Finds Moviemaking Fulfilling." *Houston Post,* March 8, 1987, sec. F, p. 3.

Martin, Carter. "Horton Foote's Southern Family in *Roots in a Parched Ground.*" *Texas Review,* XII (Spring–Summer 1991), 76–82.

McDowell, S. Dixon. "Horton Foote's Film Aesthetic." In *Horton Foote: A Casebook,* edited by Gerald C. Wood. New York, 1997, pp. 137–50.

McLaughlin, Buzz. "Conversation with Horton Foote." *Dramatists Guild Quarterly,* XXIX (Winter 1993), 17–27.

Mendell, Dean. "Squeezing the Drama out of Melodrama: Plot and Counterplot in *Laura Dennis.*" In *Horton Foote: A Casebook,* edited by Gerald C. Wood. New York, 1997, pp. 189–201.

Moore, Barbara, and David G. Yellin. Introduction to *Horton Foote's Three Trips to Bountiful.* Dallas, 1993.

Neff, David. "Going Home to the Hidden God." *Christianity Today,* April 4, 1986, pp. 30–31.

O'Driscoll, Tod. "Ways of Seeing: American Writers and Photographers in Portraits and Interviews." M.A. thesis, Regent University, 1995.

O'Quinn, Jim. "Eye of the Beholder." Interview. *American Theatre,* XII (September 1995), 22–36.

Porter, Laurin R. "An Interview with Horton Foote." *Studies in American Drama, 1945–Present,* VI (1991), 177–94.

————. "Subtext as Text: Language and Culture in Horton Foote's Texas Cycle." In *Horton Foote: A Casebook,* edited by Gerald C. Wood. New York, 1997, pp. 109–29.

Price, Reynolds. "Introduction: New Treasure" to *"Courtship," "Valentine's Day," "1918": Three Plays from "The Orphans' Home" Cycle.* New York, 1987.

Reinert, Al. "Tender Foote: Horton Foote Continues to Find Big Themes in Small-town Life." *Texas Monthly,* July 1991, pp. 110, 132–37.

Rich, Frank. "Stage: In Marathon '85, 'Road to the Graveyard.' " *New York Times,* May 27, 1985, p. 11.

Roberts, Jerry. "Horton Foote and *Tomorrow.*" Interview. In *Movie Talk from the Front Lines: Filmmakers Discuss Their Works with the Los Angeles Film Critics Association.* Jefferson, N.C., 1995.

Seidenberg, Robert. "Period Perfect: Van Broughton Ramsey Costumes Horton Foote's Texas." *Theatre Crafts,* May 1987, pp. 99–102.

Shackelford, Dean. "The Female Voice in *To Kill a Mockingbird*: Narrative Strategies in Film and Novel." *Mississippi Quarterly,* L (Winter 1996–97), 101–13.

Simon, John. "Theater." *New York,* September 28, 1992, p. 54.

Skaggs, Calvin. "Interview with Horton Foote." In *The American Short Story,* edited by Calvin Skaggs. New York, 1977.

Skaggs, Merrill Maquire. "The Story and Film of *Barn Burning.*" *Southern Quarterly,* XXI (Winter 1983), 5–15.

Smelstor, Marjorie. " 'The World's an Orphans' Home': Horton Foote's Social and Moral History." *Southern Quarterly,* XIX (Winter 1991), 7–16.

Smith, Amanda. "Horton Foote: A Writer's Journey." *Varia,* July–August 1987, pp. 18–20, 23, 26–27.

Sterritt, David. "Horton Foote: Filmmaking Radical with a Tender Touch." *Christian Science Monitor,* May 15, 1986, pp. 1, 36.

———. "Let's Hear It for the Human Being." *Saturday Evening Post,* October 1983, pp. 36–38.

Tanner, Louise. "An Interview with Horton Foote." *Films in Review,* XXXVII (November 1986), 530–31.

Teicholz, Tom. "Screenwriters: Horton Foote." *Interview,* September 1985, pp. 264–65.

Torrens, James S. "Two by Horton Foote." *America,* December 17, 1994, p. 21.

Townsend, Jarrod Terence. "From Page to Stage: Directing Horton Foote's *Courtship* from *The Orphans' Home* Cycle." M.A. thesis, Arizona State University, 1994.

Underwood, Susan. "Singing in the Face of Devastation: Texture in Horton Foote's *Talking Pictures.*" In *Horton Foote: A Casebook,* edited by Gerald C. Wood. New York, 1997, pp. 151–62.

Wall, James M. "Home, Family, Religion." *Christian Century,* February 19, 1997, pp. 179–80.

———. "Independent Visions." *Christian Century,* November 19, 1997, pp. 1059–60.

Watson, Charles S. "Beyond the Commercial Media: Horton Foote's Procession of Defeated Men." *Studies in American Drama, 1945–Present,* VIII (1993), 175–87.

———. "Past and Present Cultures in Recent Drama." In *The History of Southern Drama.* Lexington, Ky., 1997, pp. 192–201.

Wood, Gerald C. "Boundaries, the Female Will, and Individuation in *Night Seasons.*" In *Horton Foote: A Casebook,* edited by Gerald C. Wood. New York, 1997, pp. 163–77.

———. "Horton Foote: An Interview." *Post Script,* X (Summer 1991), 3–12.

———. "Horton Foote's Politics of Intimacy." *Journal of American Drama and Theatre,* IX (Spring 1997), 44–57.

———. Introduction to *Horton Foote: A Casebook.* Edited by Gerald C. Wood. New York, 1997, pp. 1–6.

———. Introduction to *Selected One-Acts,* xiii–xxii.

———. "The Nature of Mystery in *The Young Man from Atlanta.*" In *Horton Foote: A Casebook,* edited by Gerald C. Wood. New York, 1997, pp. 179–88.

———. "Old Beginnings and Roads to Home: Horton Foote and Mythic Realism." *Christianity and Literature,* XLV (Spring–Summer 1996), 359–72.

———, ed. *Horton Foote: A Casebook.* New York, 1997.

———, ed. *Selected One-Act Plays of Horton Foote.* Dallas, 1989.

Wood, Gerald C., and Terry Barr. " 'A Certain Kind of Writer': An Interview with Horton Foote." *Literature/Film Quarterly,* XIV (1986), 226–37.

Wright, Tim. "Dancing with Shadows: Stylistic Attributes of Impressionism in Selected Works by Horton Foote." Ph.D. dissertation, Regent University, 1995.

———. "More Real Than Realism: Horton Foote's Impressionism." In *Horton Foote: A Casebook,* edited by Gerald C. Wood. New York, 1997, pp. 67–87.

Yellin, David, and Marie Connors. "Faulkner and Foote and Chemistry." In *Tomorrow and Tomorrow and Tomorrow,* edited by David G. Yellin and Marie Connors. Jackson, Miss., 1985.

Young, Stark. Foreword to *The Traveling Lady,* by Horton Foote. New York, 1955.

Young, Stephen Flinn. "A Conversation with Dixon McDowell: The Horton Foote Documentary." *Southern Quarterly,* XXXII (Spring 1994), 147–57.

Young, Wendy Ann. "The Role of Elizabeth in Horton Foote's *1918:* A Production Thesis in Acting." M.F.A. thesis, Louisiana State University, 1990.

OTHER WORKS CITED

Barthes, Roland. "Myth Today." In *A Barthes Reader,* edited by Susan Sontag. New York, 1982.

Bigsby, C. W. E. *Modern American Drama, 1945–90.* New York, 1992.

Brustein, Robert. *Reimagining American Theatre.* New York, 1991.

Campbell, Joseph. "Mythological Themes in Creative Literature and Art." In *Myths, Dreams, and Religions,* edited by Joseph Campbell. New York, 1970.

Christian Science: A Sourcebook of Contemporary Materials. Boston, 1990.

de Mille, Agnes. *Martha: The Life and Work of Martha Graham.* New York, 1991.

Doyle, Patricia Martin. "Women and Religion: Psychological and Cultural Implications." In *Religion and Sexism: Images of Woman in the Jewish and Christian Traditions,* edited by Rosemary Radford Ruether. New York, 1974.

Eddy, Mary Baker. *Science and Health with Key to the Scriptures.* Boston, 1934.

Eliade, Mircea. *Myth and Reality.* Translated by Willard R. Trask. New York, 1963.

———. *The Myth of the Eternal Return.* Translated by Willard R. Trask. New York, 1965.

Engelsman, Joan Chamberlain. *The Feminine Dimension of the Divine*. Philadelphia, 1979.

Erikson, Erik. *Identity: Youth and Crisis*. New York, 1968.

Gottschalk, Stephen. "Christian Science." In *The Encyclopedia of Religion*, edited by Mircea Eliade. Vol. III. New York, 1987.

————. *The Emergence of Christian Science in American Religious Life*. Berkeley, 1973.

————. "Theodicy after Auschwitz and the Reality of God." *Union Seminary Quarterly Review*, XLI (1987), 77–91.

Goyen, William. *The House of Breath*. New York, 1949.

Greeley, Andrew M. *The Mary Myth: On the Femininity of God*. New York, 1977.

Hirsch, Foster. *A Method to Their Madness: The History of the Actors Studio*. New York, 1984.

Horwitz, Dawn Lille. "Modern Dance." In *The Dance Catalog*, edited by Nancy Reynolds. New York, 1979.

Humphrey, Doris. *The Art of Making Dances*. New York, 1959.

Johnson, Elizabeth. *She Who Is: The Mystery of God in Feminist Theological Discourse*. New York, 1992.

Maguire, Daniel C. "The Feminization of God and Ethics." *Christianity and Crisis*, XLII (March 15, 1982), 59–67.

Martin, John. *America Dancing*. New York, 1936.

May, Rollo. *The Cry for Myth*. New York, 1991.

Mollenkott, Virginia Ramey. *The Divine Feminine: The Biblical Imagery of God as Female*. New York, 1983.

O'Connor, Flannery. *Mystery and Manners*. Selected and edited by Sally and Robert Fitzgerald. New York, 1980.

Ortega y Gasset, José. *The Dehumanization of Art and Other Essays on Art, Culture, and Literature*. Princeton, 1968.

————. *Phenomenology and Art*. New York, 1975.

Peel, Robert. *Health and Medicine in the Christian Science Tradition*. New York, 1988.

————. *Mary Baker Eddy: The Years of Authority*. New York, 1977.

————. *Mary Baker Eddy: The Years of Discovery*. New York, 1966.

————. *Mary Baker Eddy: The Years of Trial*. New York, 1971.

Porter, Katherine Anne. *The Collected Essays and Occasional Writings of Katherine Anne Porter*. Boston, 1970.

Robinson, Marc. *The Other American Drama*. New York, 1994.

Romero, Joan Arnold. "The Protestant Principle: A Woman's-Eye View of Barth and Tillich." In *Religion and Sexism: Images of Woman in the Jewish and Christian Traditions,* edited by Rosemary Radford Ruether. New York, 1974.

Ruether, Rosemary Radford. *Mary—The Feminine Face of the Church*. Philadelphia, 1977.

———. *Sexism and God-Talk: Toward a Feminist Theology*. Boston, 1983.

Simpson, Lewis. *The Fable of the Southern Writer*. Baton Rouge, 1994.

Spears, Ross. "Regional Filmmaking: The James Agee Film Project." *Southern Quarterly*, XIX (Spring–Summer 1981), 223–25.

Thompson, Barbara. "Katherine Anne Porter." In *Writers at Work: The Paris Review Interviews*. 2d series. New York, 1963.

Tillich, Paul. *The Courage to Be*. New Haven, 1952.

Wilson-Kastner, Patricia. *Faith, Feminism, and the Christ*. Philadelphia, 1983.

Zikmund, Barbara Brown. "The Feminist Thrust of Sectarian Christianity." In *Women of Spirit: Female Leadership in the Jewish and Christian Traditions,* edited by Rosemary Ruether and Eleanor McLaughlin. New York, 1979.

Index